Ripley's
Believe It or Not!®

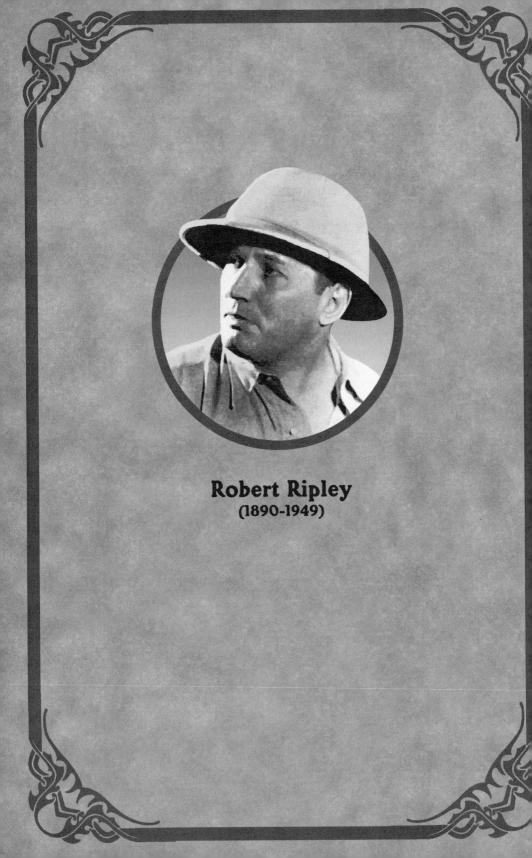

Robert Ripley
(1890-1949)

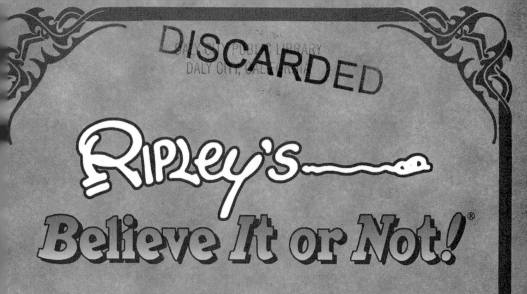

Ripley's Believe It or Not!

Script
Haden Blackman

Pencils
Cary Nord

Inks
Mark Lipka

Letters
Steve Dutro

Cover Artist
Cary Nord

Cover Colors
Dan Jackson

DARK HORSE COMICS®

B

Table of Contents

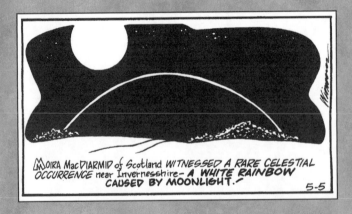

MOIRA MacDIARMID of Scotland WITNESSED A RARE CELESTIAL OCCURRENCE near Invernesshire- A WHITE RAINBOW CAUSED BY MOONLIGHT.

5-5

Publisher • **Mike Richardson**
Editor • **Dave Land**
Assistant Editor • **Philip W. Simon**
Collection Designer • **Debra Bailey**
Art Director • **Mark Cox**

This book collects issues 1 through 3 of the Dark Horse comic-book
series Ripley's Believe It or Not!

Dark Horse Comics, Inc.
10956 SE Main Street
Milwaukie, OR 97222

www.darkhorse.com

To find a comic shop in your area, call the Comic Shop Locator Service
toll-free at (888) 266-4226

First edition: May 2003
ISBN: 1-56971-909-8

1 3 5 7 9 10 8 6 4 2

Printed in Canada

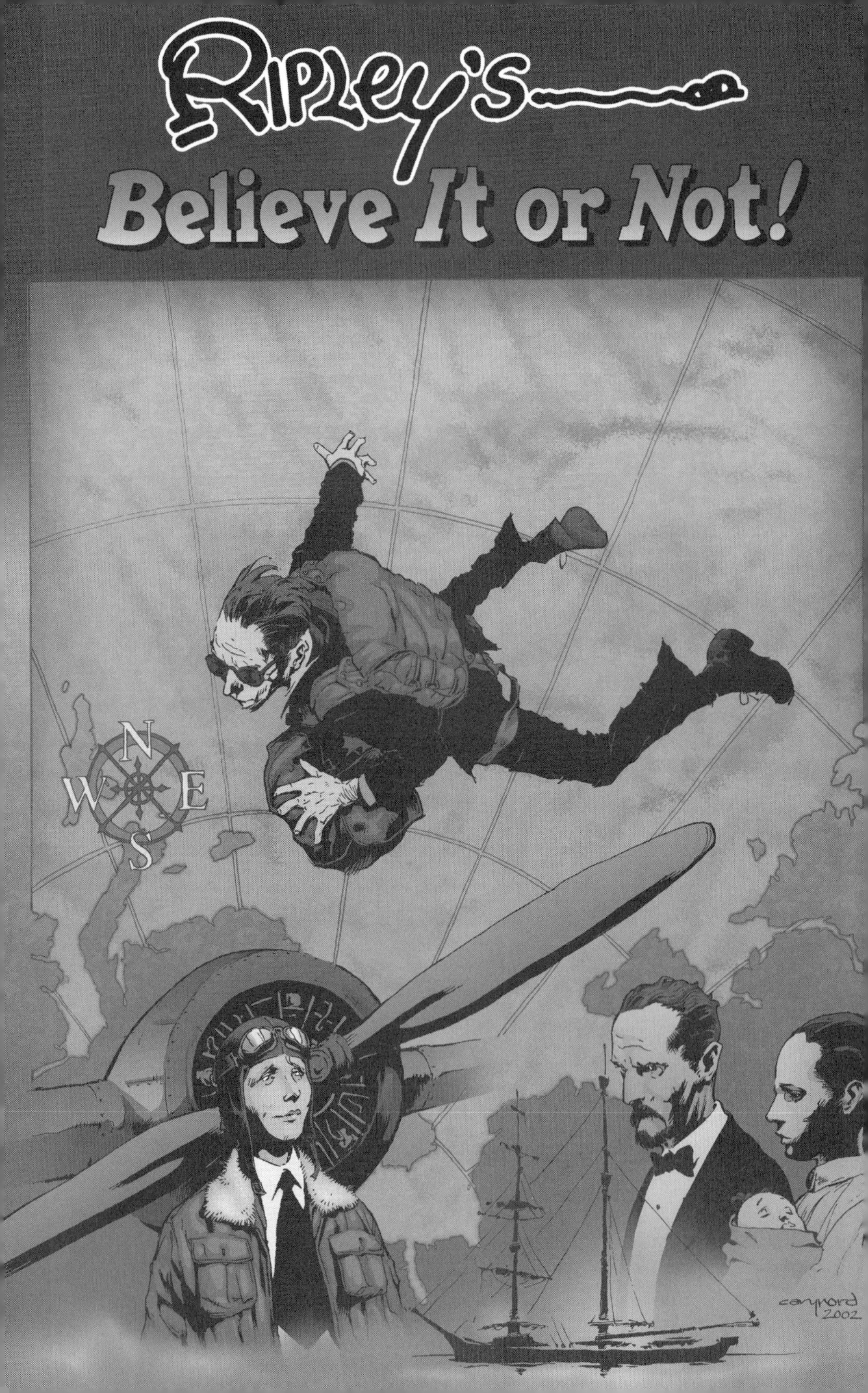
Ripley's
Believe It or Not!
N
W
E
S

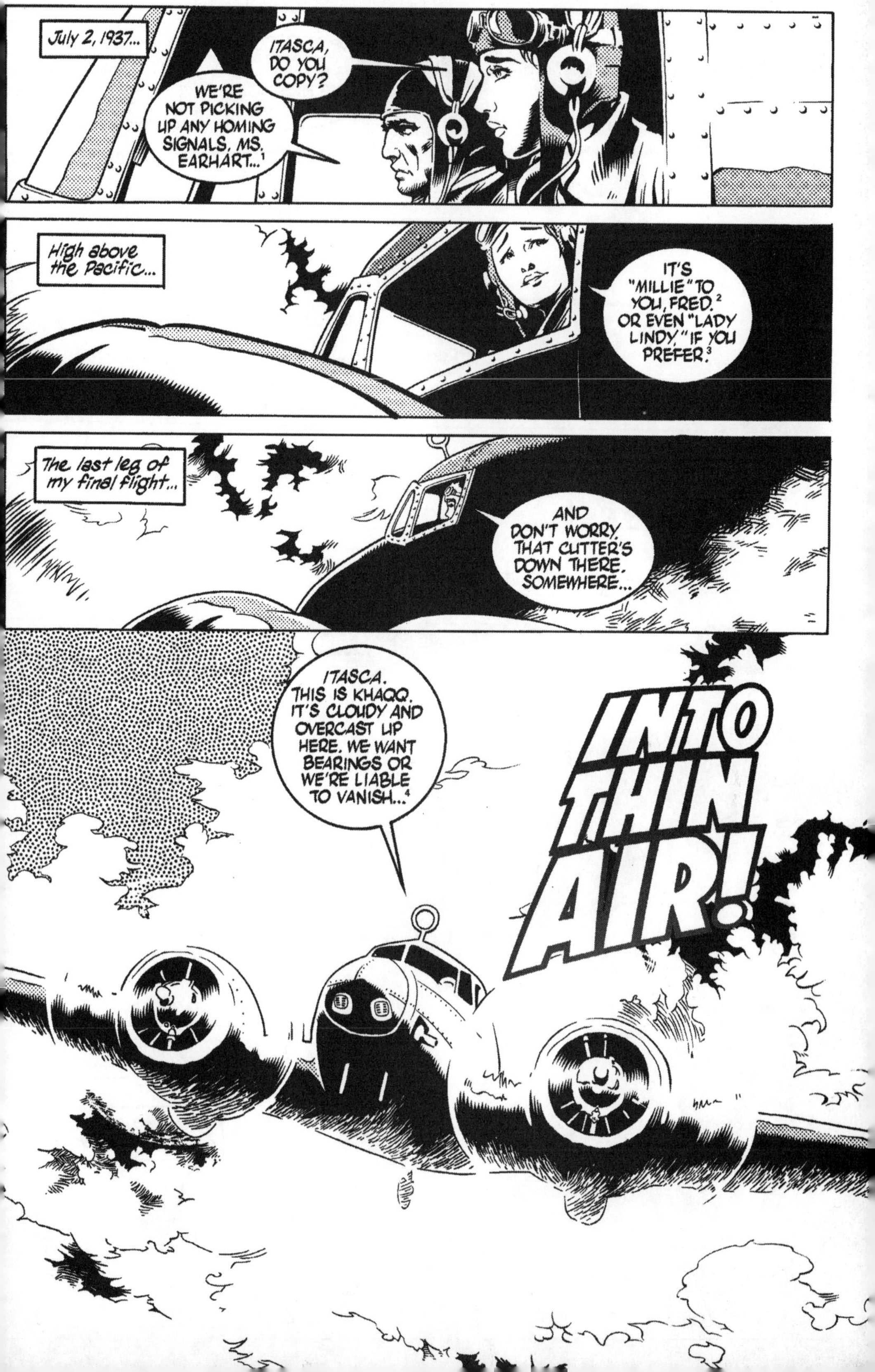
July 2, 1937...
ITASCA, DO YOU COPY?
WE'RE NOT PICKING UP ANY HOMING SIGNALS, MS. EARHART...[1]
High above the Pacific...
IT'S "MILLIE" TO YOU, FRED.[2] OR EVEN "LADY LINDY," IF YOU PREFER.[3]
The last leg of my final flight...
AND DON'T WORRY. THAT CUTTER'S DOWN THERE. SOMEWHERE...
ITASCA. THIS IS KHAQQ. IT'S CLOUDY AND OVERCAST UP HERE. WE WANT BEARINGS OR WE'RE LIABLE TO VANISH...[4]
INTO THIN AIR!

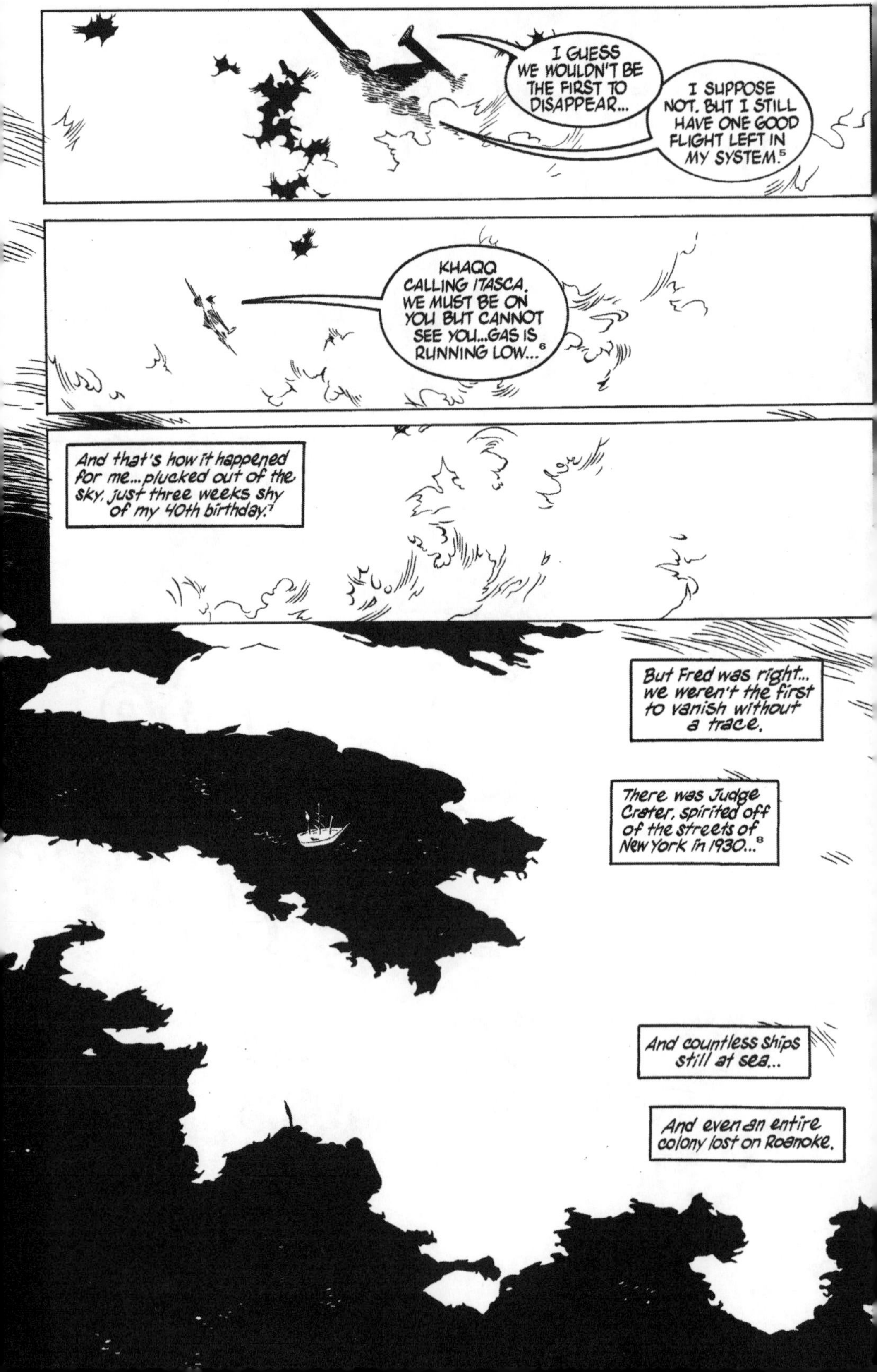
I GUESS WE WOULDN'T BE THE FIRST TO DISAPPEAR...
I SUPPOSE NOT. BUT I STILL HAVE ONE GOOD FLIGHT LEFT IN MY SYSTEM.[5]
KHAQQ CALLING ITASCA. WE MUST BE ON YOU BUT CANNOT SEE YOU...GAS IS RUNNING LOW...[6]
And that's how it happened for me...plucked out of the sky, just three weeks shy of my 40th birthday.[7]
But Fred was right... we weren't the first to vanish without a trace.
There was Judge Crater, spirited off of the streets of New York in 1930...[8]
And countless ships still at sea...
And even an entire colony lost on Roanoke.

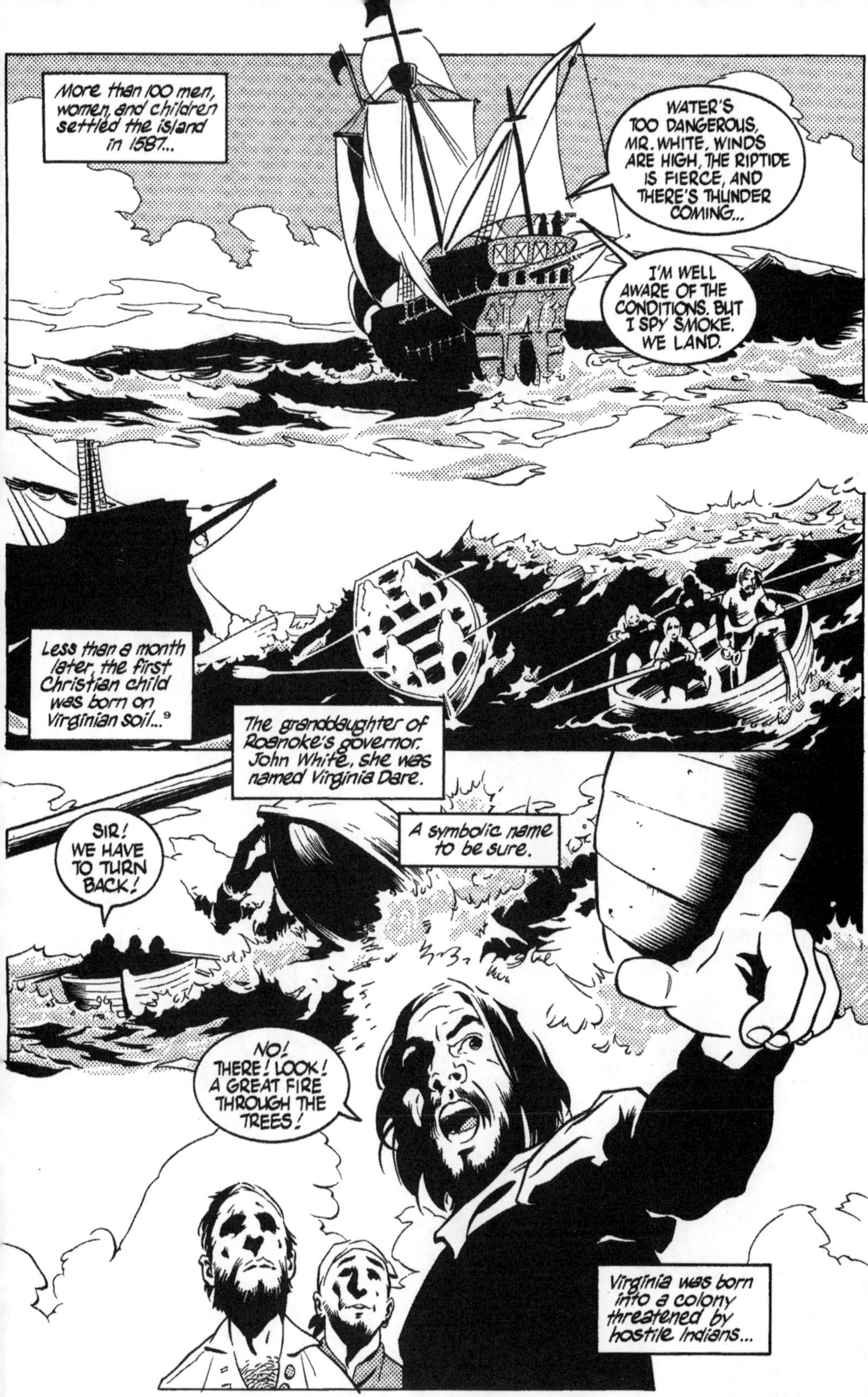
More than 100 men, women, and children settled the island in 1587...
WATER'S TOO DANGEROUS, MR. WHITE. WINDS ARE HIGH, THE RIPTIDE IS FIERCE, AND THERE'S THUNDER COMING...
I'M WELL AWARE OF THE CONDITIONS. BUT I SPY SMOKE. WE LAND.
Less than a month later, the first Christian child was born on Virginian soil...⁹
The granddaughter of Roanoke's governor, John White, she was named Virginia Dare.
SIR! WE HAVE TO TURN BACK!
A symbolic name to be sure.
NO! THERE! LOOK! A GREAT FIRE THROUGH THE TREES!
Virginia was born into a colony threatened by hostile Indians...

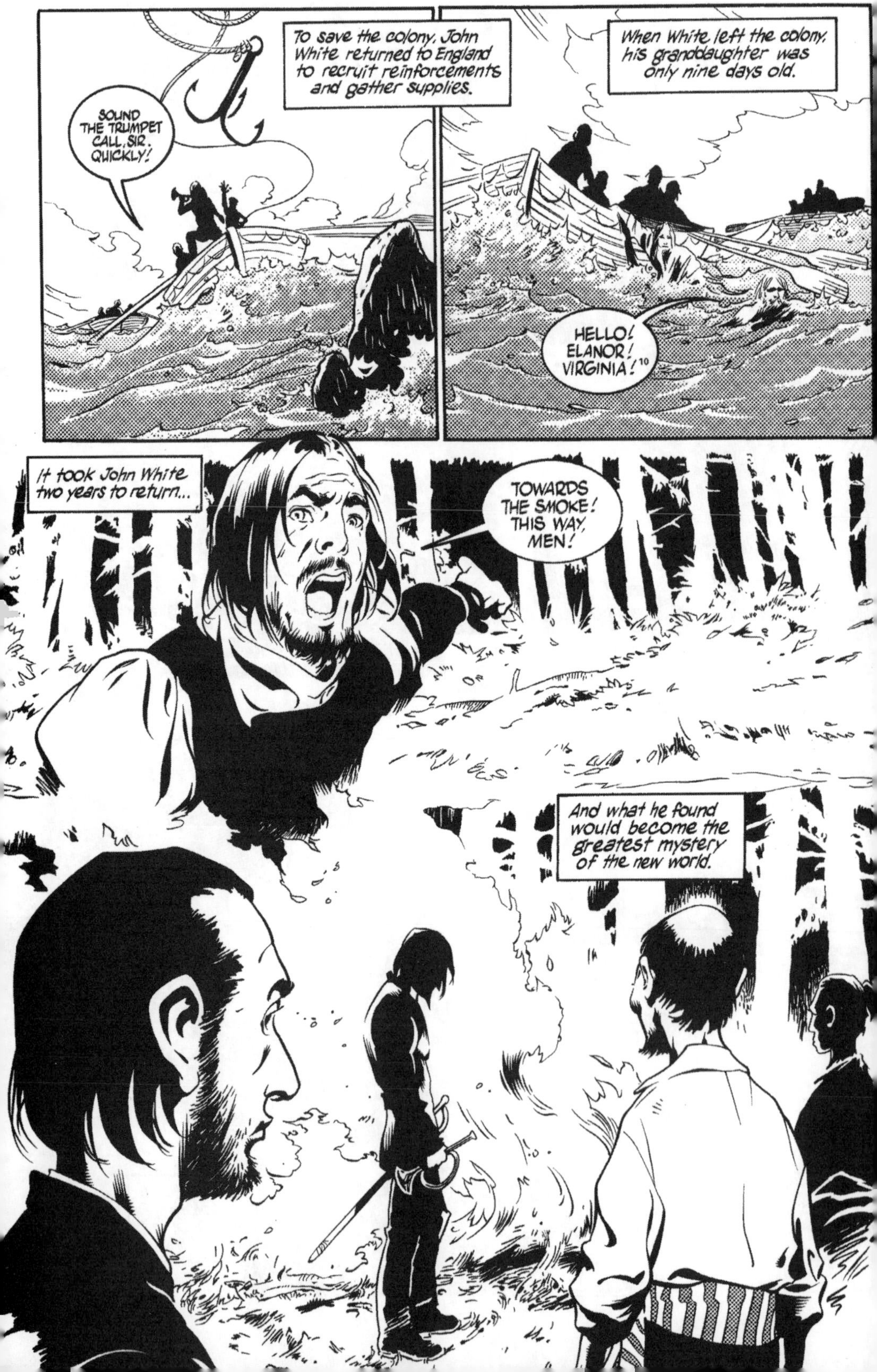
To save the colony, John White returned to England to recruit reinforcements and gather supplies.
SOUND THE TRUMPET CALL, SIR. QUICKLY!
When White left the colony, his granddaughter was only nine days old.
HELLO! ELANOR! VIRGINIA![10]
It took John White two years to return...
TOWARDS THE SMOKE! THIS WAY, MEN!
And what he found would become the greatest mystery of the new world.

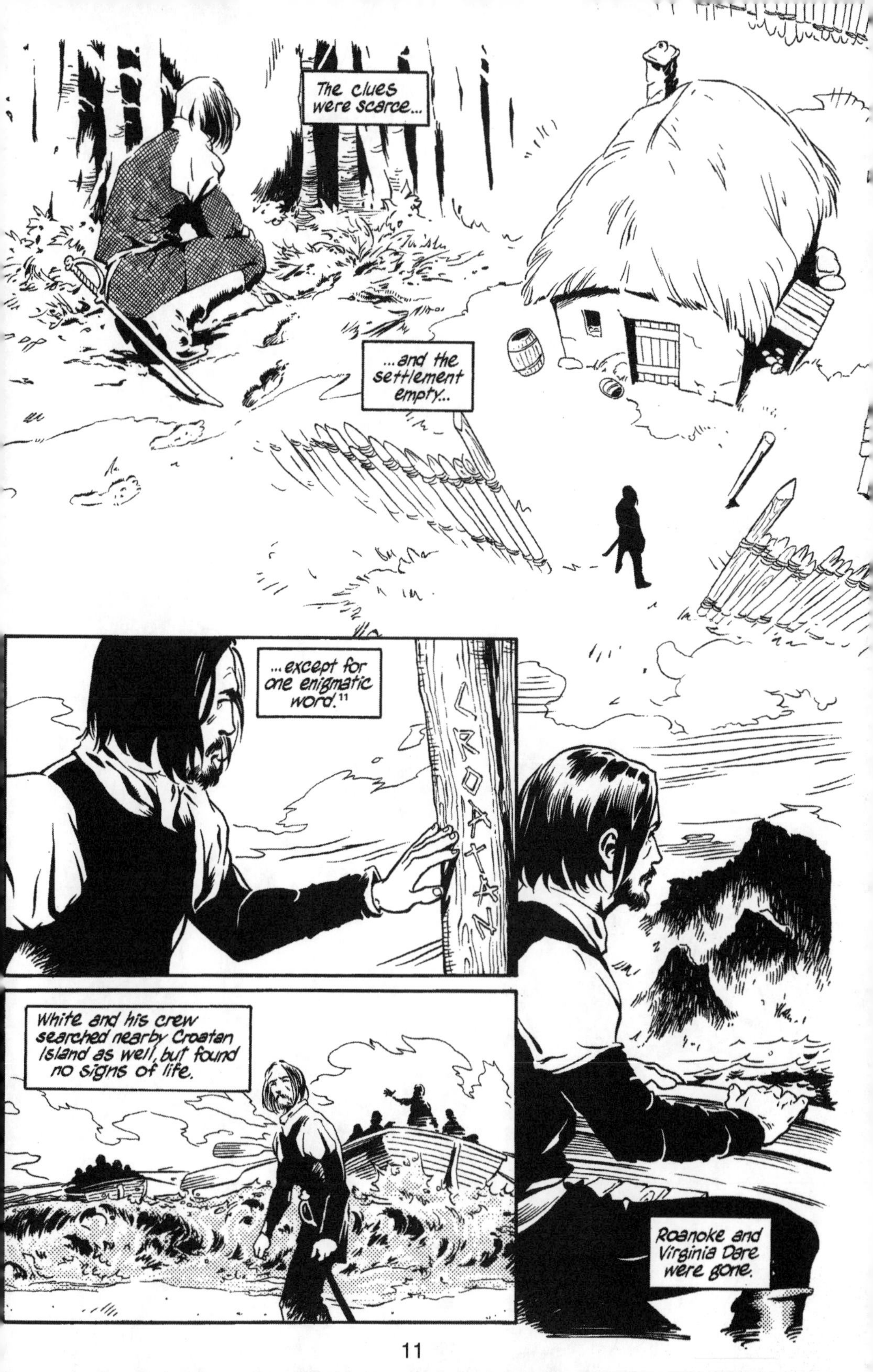
The clues were scarce...
...and the settlement empty...
...except for one enigmatic word.[11]
CROATAN
White and his crew searched nearby Croatan Island as well, but found no signs of life.
Roanoke and Virginia Dare were gone.

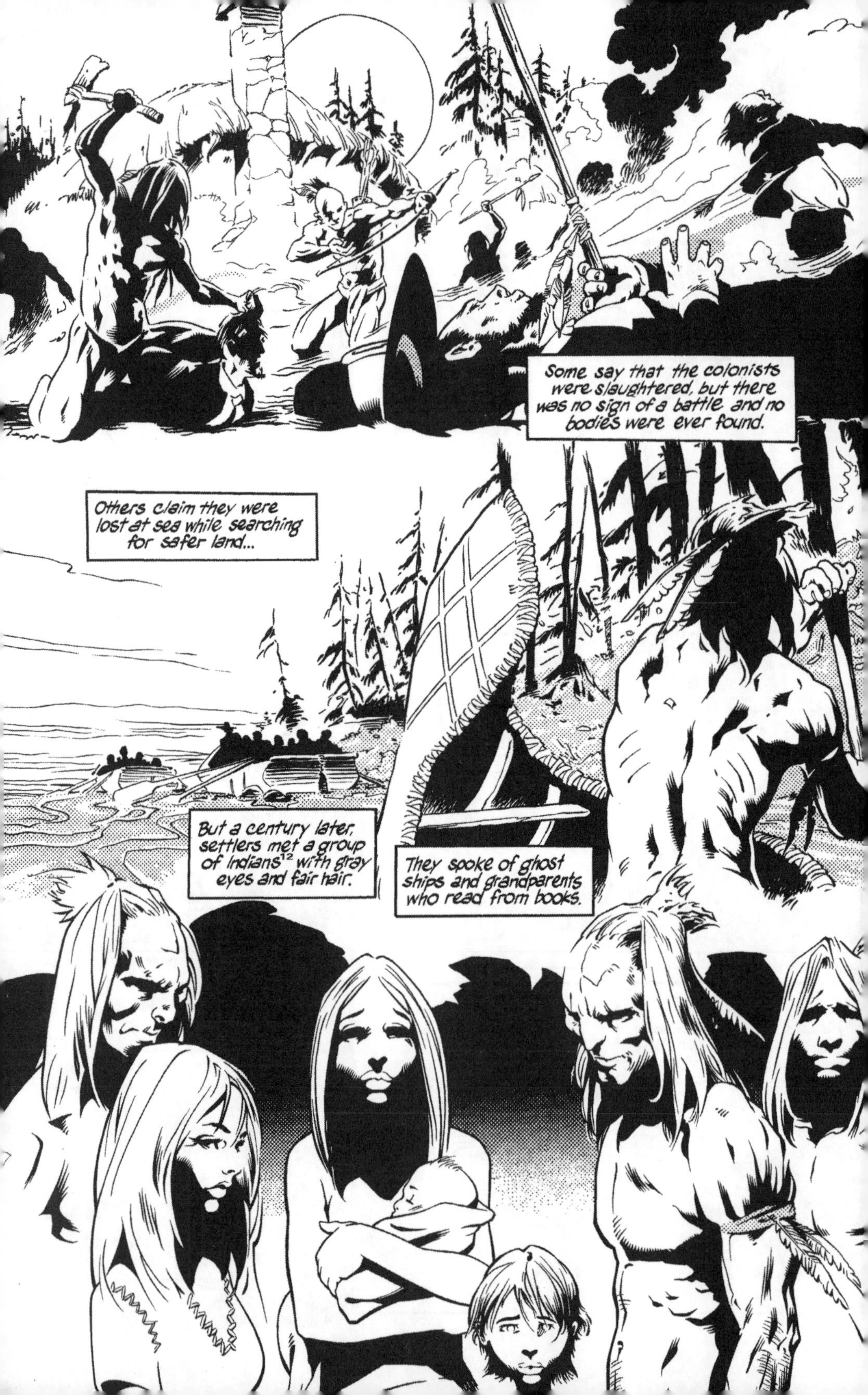
Some say that the colonists were slaughtered, but there was no sign of a battle and no bodies were ever found.
Others claim they were lost at sea while searching for safer land...
But a century later, settlers met a group of Indians[12] with gray eyes and fair hair.
They spoke of ghost ships and grandparents who read from books.

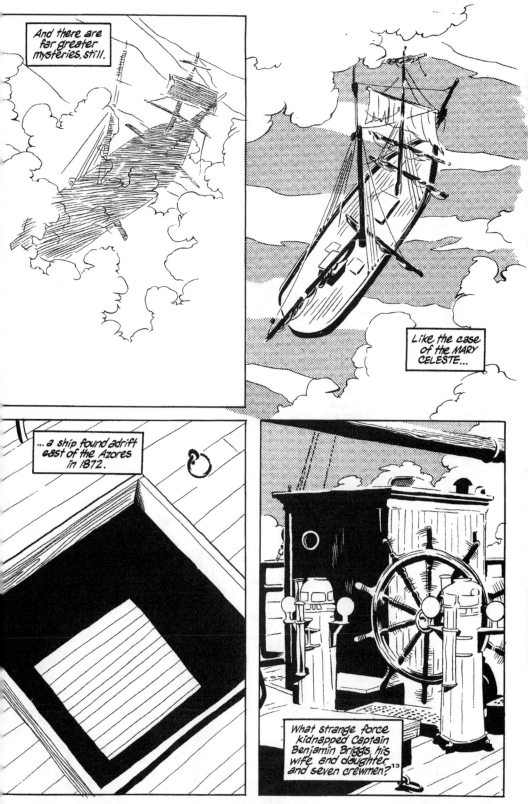

And there are far greater mysteries, still.

Like the case of the MARY CELESTE...

...a ship found adrift east of the Azores in 1872.

What strange force kidnapped Captain Benjamin Briggs, his wife and daughter, and seven crewmen?[13]

13

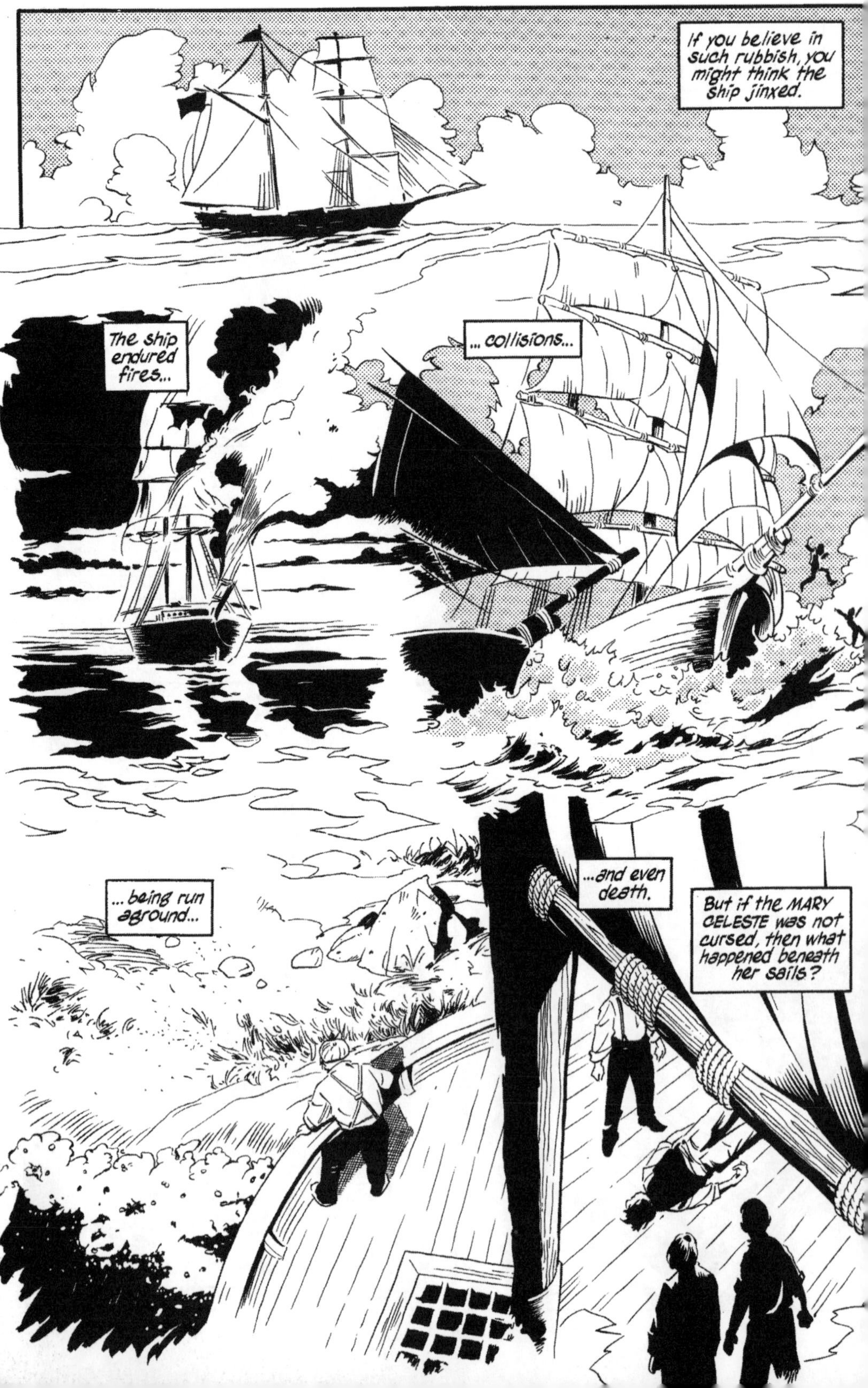
If you believe in such rubbish, you might think the ship jinxed.
The ship endured fires...
...collisions...
...being run aground...
...and even death.
But if the MARY CELESTE was not cursed, then what happened beneath her sails?

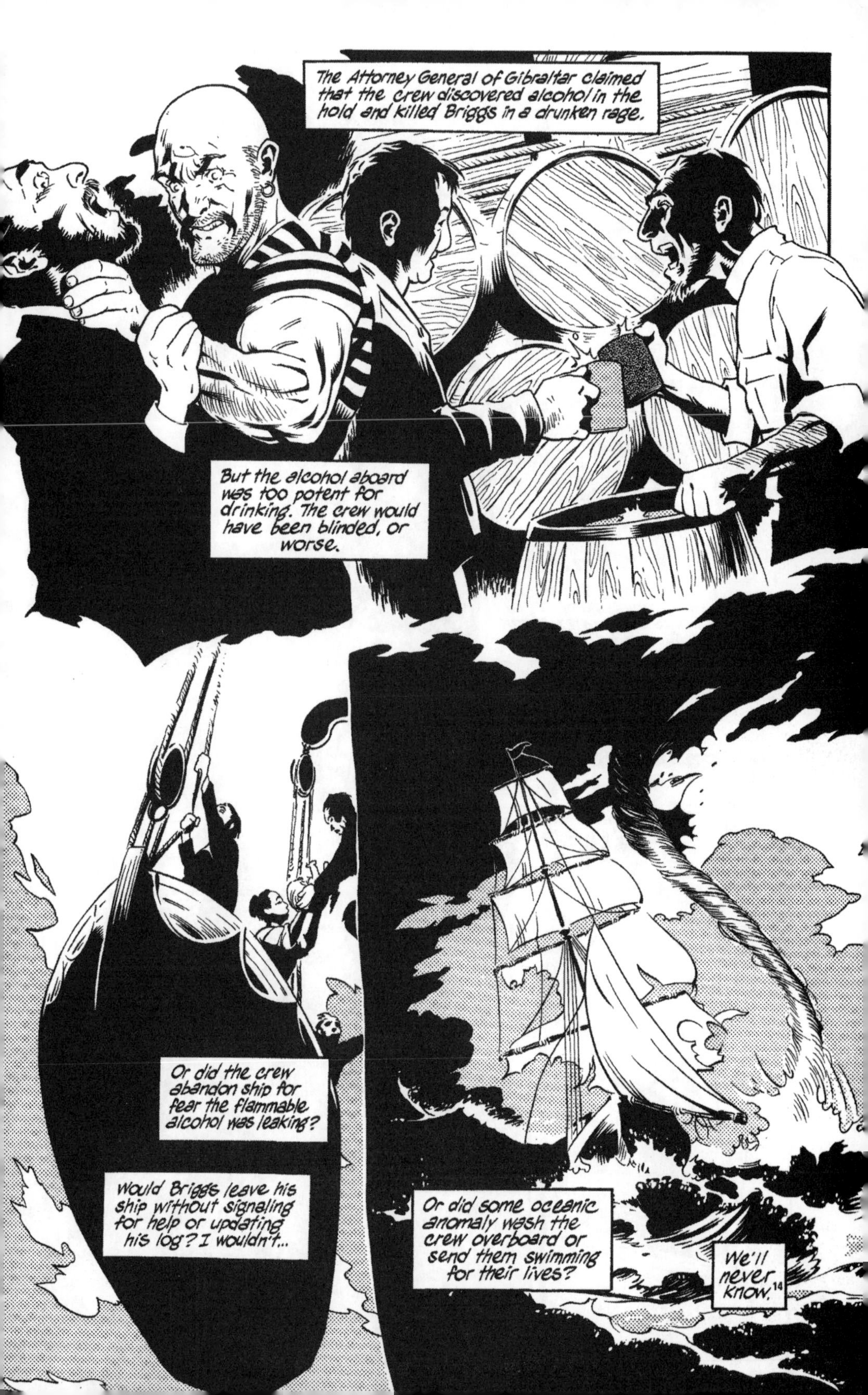
The Attorney General of Gibraltar claimed that the crew discovered alcohol in the hold and killed Briggs in a drunken rage.
But the alcohol aboard was too potent for drinking. The crew would have been blinded, or worse.
Or did the crew abandon ship for fear the flammable alcohol was leaking?
Would Briggs leave his ship without signaling for help or updating his log? I wouldn't...
Or did some oceanic anomaly wash the crew overboard or send them swimming for their lives?
We'll never know.[14]

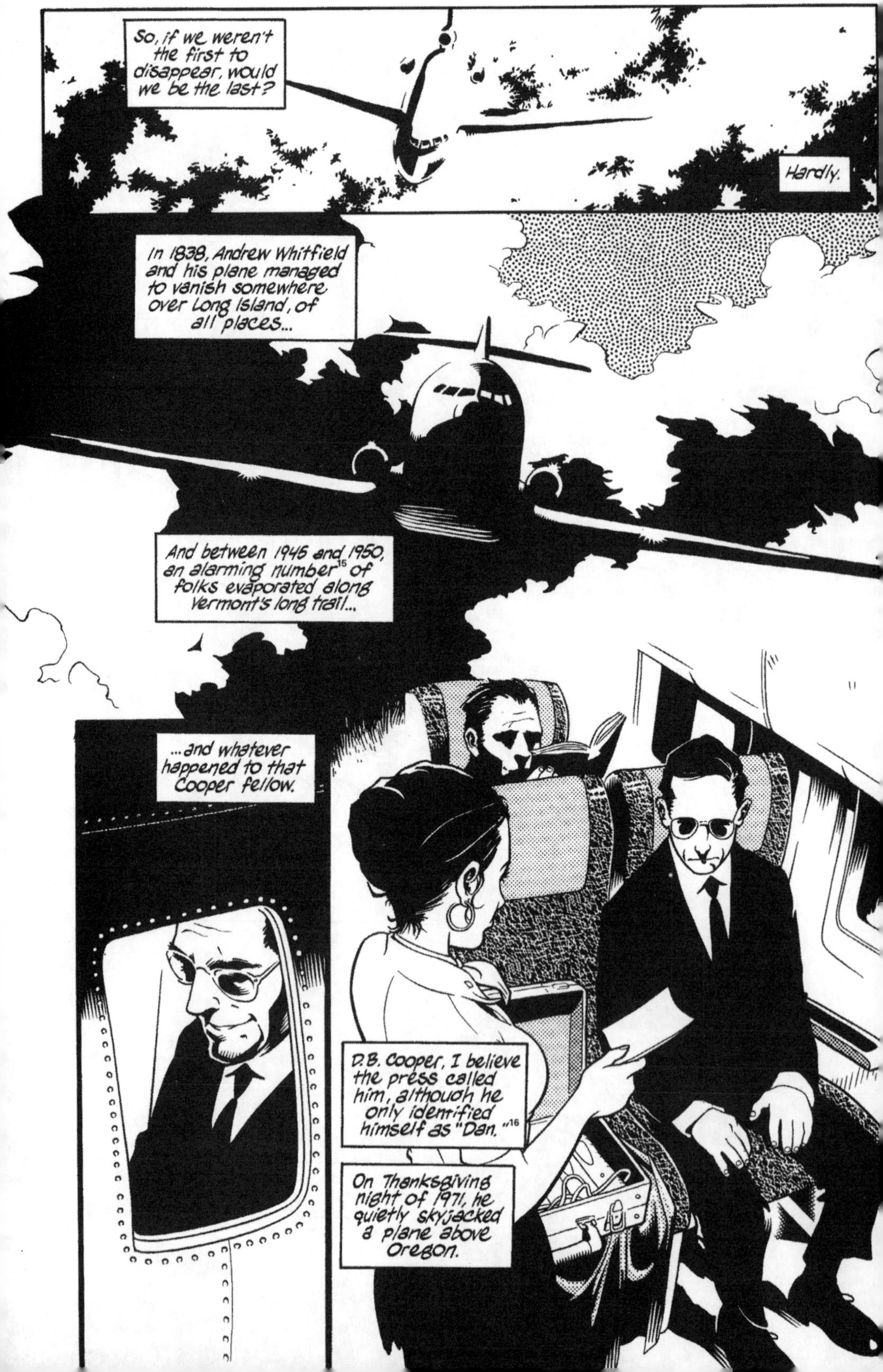
So, if we weren't the first to disappear, would we be the last?
Hardly.
In 1838, Andrew Whitfield and his plane managed to vanish somewhere over Long Island, of all places...
And between 1946 and 1950, an alarming number[15] of folks evaporated along Vermont's long trail...
...and whatever happened to that Cooper fellow.
D.B. Cooper, I believe the press called him, although he only identified himself as "Dan."[16]
On Thanksgiving night of 1971, he quietly skyjacked a plane above Oregon.

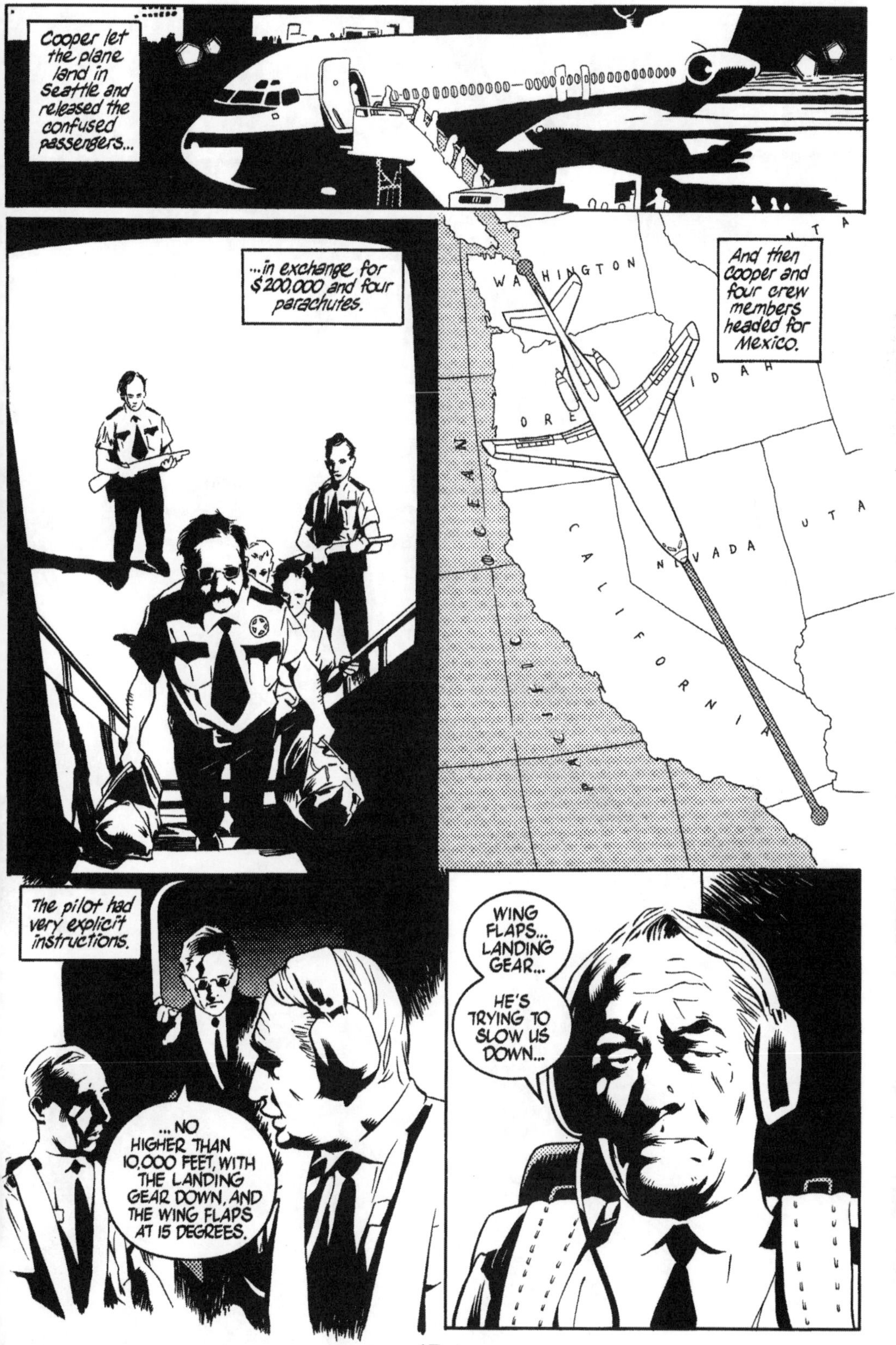
Cooper let the plane land in Seattle and released the confused passengers...
...in exchange for $200,000 and four parachutes.
And then Cooper and four crew members headed for Mexico.
WASHINGTON
OREGON
IDAHO
NEVADA
UTAH
CALIFORNIA
PACIFIC OCEAN
The pilot had very explicit instructions.
...NO HIGHER THAN 10,000 FEET, WITH THE LANDING GEAR DOWN, AND THE WING FLAPS AT 15 DEGREES.
WING FLAPS... LANDING GEAR...
HE'S TRYING TO SLOW US DOWN...

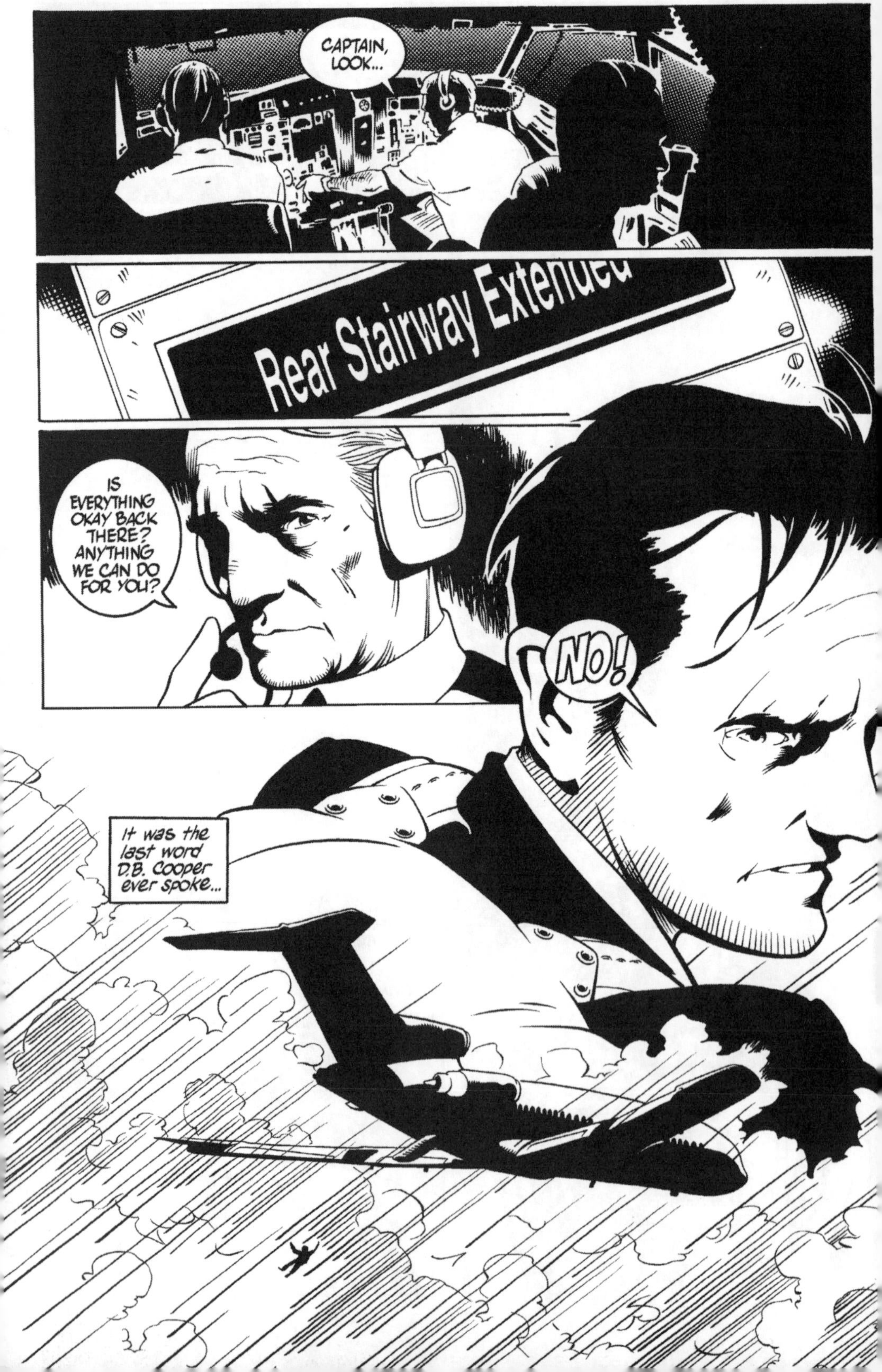
CAPTAIN, LOOK...
Rear Stairway Extended
IS EVERYTHING OKAY BACK THERE? ANYTHING WE CAN DO FOR YOU?
NO!
It was the last word D.B. Cooper ever spoke...

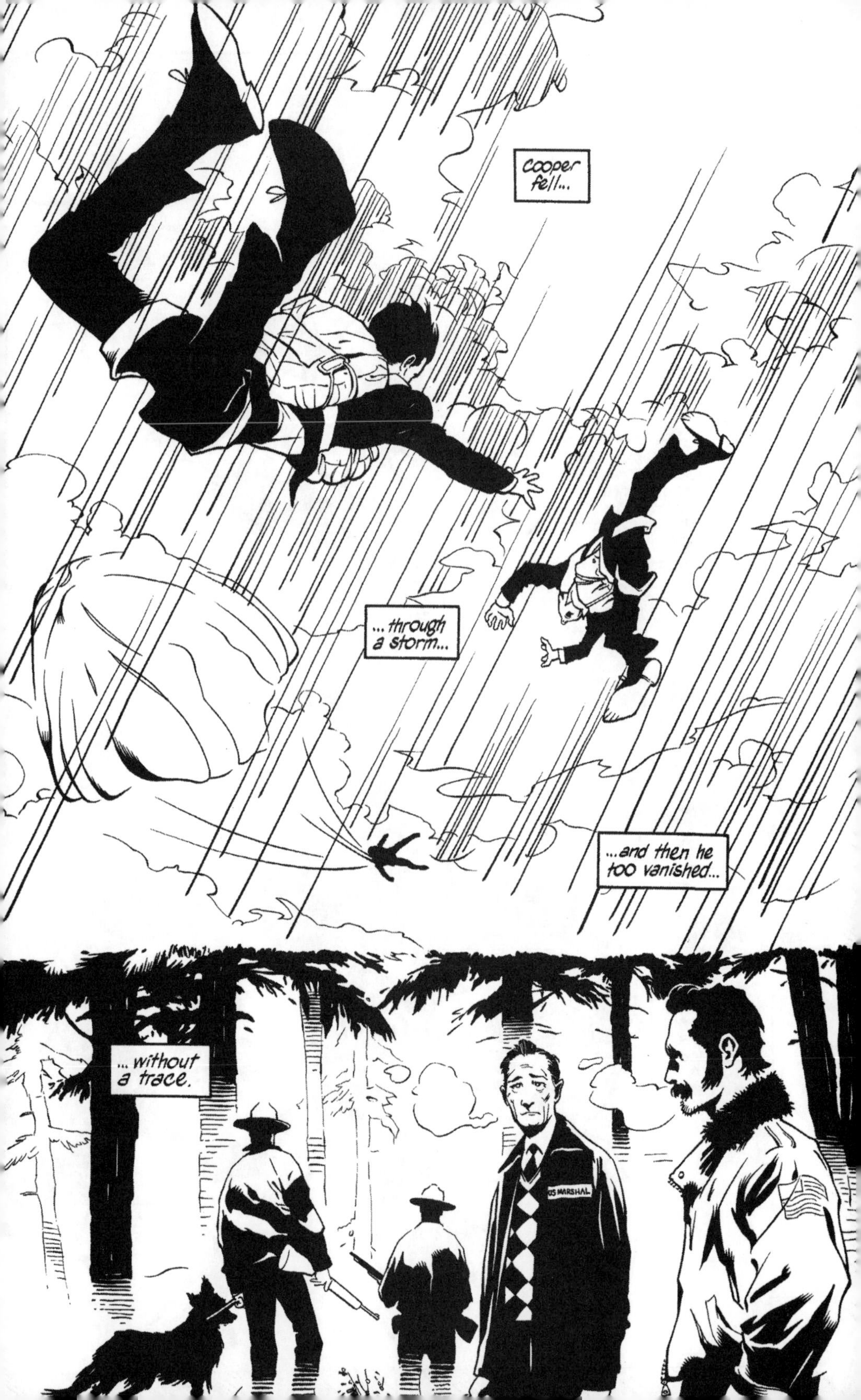
cooper fell...
...through a storm...
...and then he too vanished...
...without a trace.
US MARSHAL

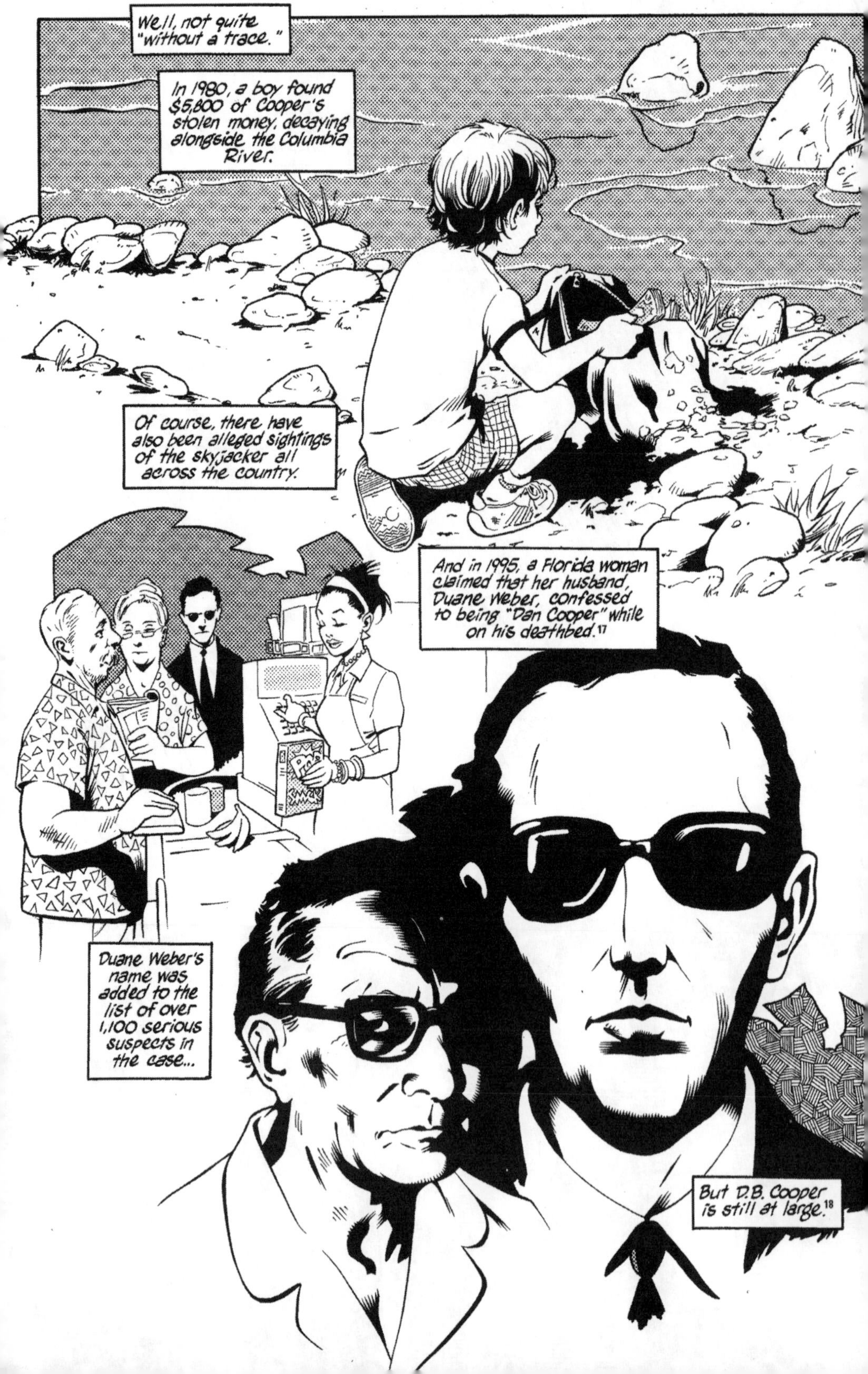
Well, not quite "without a trace."
In 1980, a boy found $5,800 of Cooper's stolen money, decaying alongside the Columbia River.
Of course, there have also been alleged sightings of the skyjacker all across the country.
And in 1995, a Florida woman claimed that her husband, Duane Weber, confessed to being "Dan Cooper" while on his deathbed.[17]
Duane Weber's name was added to the list of over 1,100 serious suspects in the case...
But D.B. Cooper is still at large.[18]

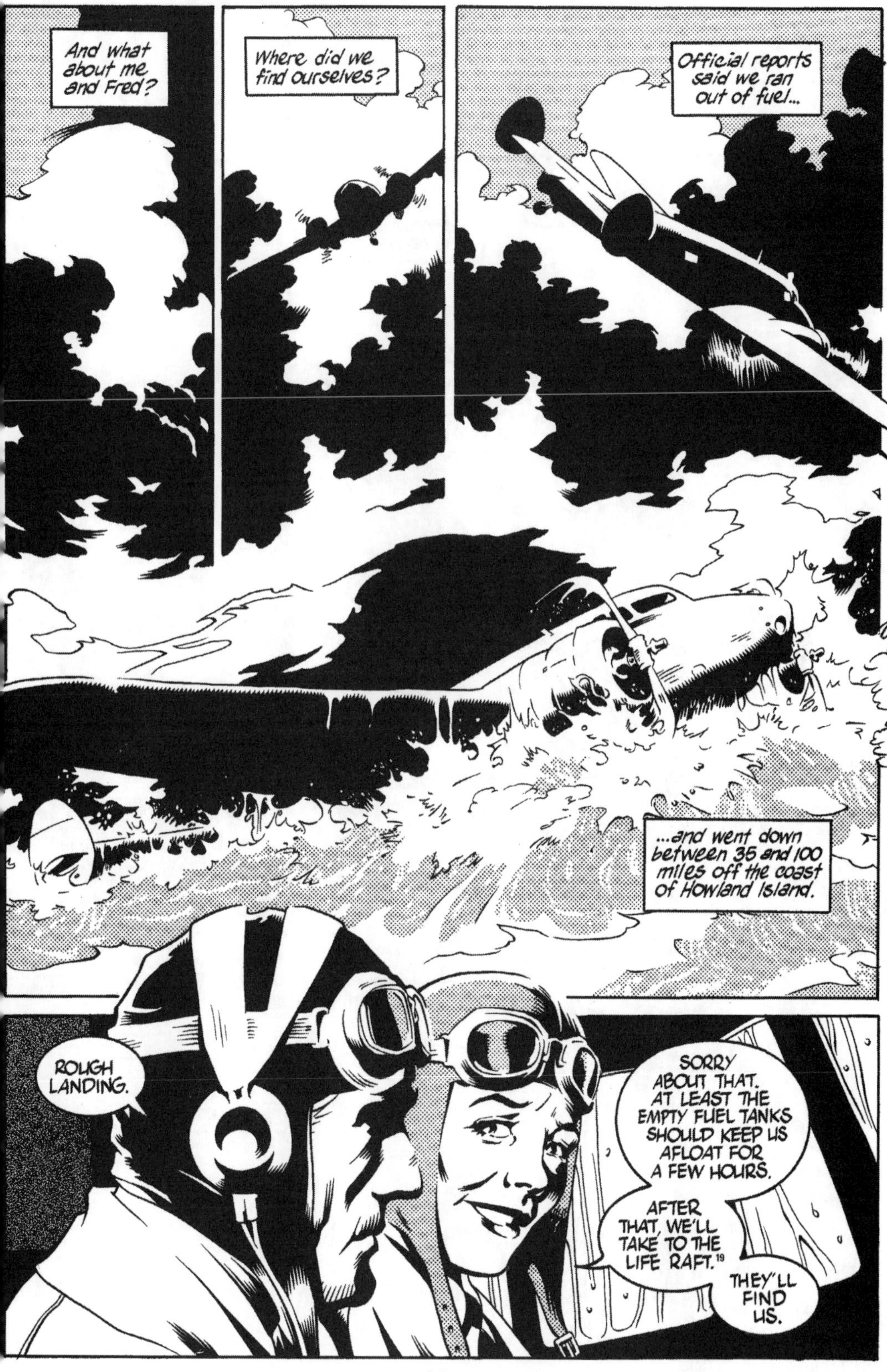
And what about me and Fred?
Where did we find ourselves?
Official reports said we ran out of fuel...
...and went down between 35 and 100 miles off the coast of Howland Island.
ROUGH LANDING.
SORRY ABOUT THAT. AT LEAST THE EMPTY FUEL TANKS SHOULD KEEP US AFLOAT FOR A FEW HOURS.
AFTER THAT, WE'LL TAKE TO THE LIFE RAFT.[19]
THEY'LL FIND US.

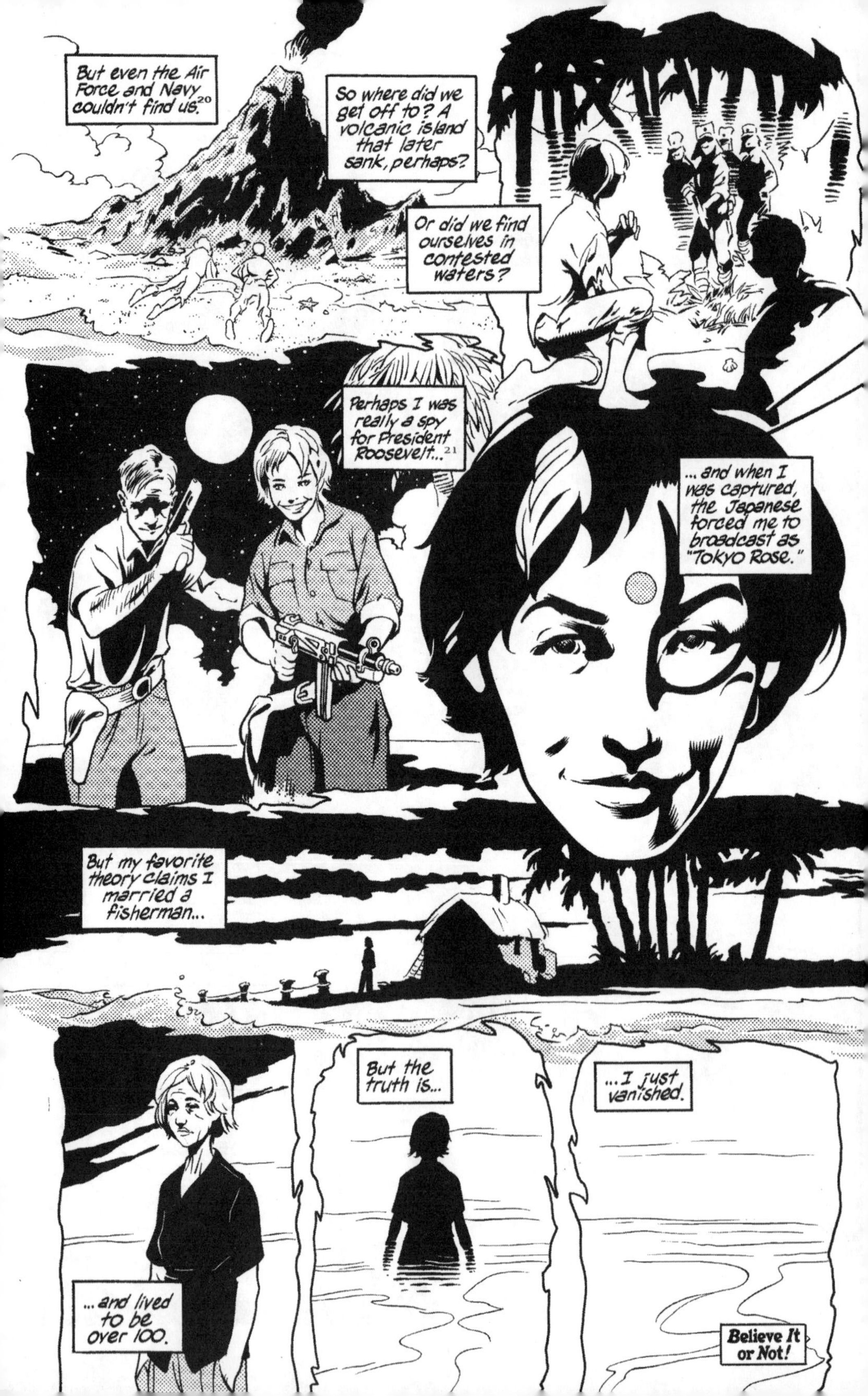
But even the Air Force and Navy couldn't find us.[20]
So where did we get off to? A volcanic island that later sank, perhaps?
Or did we find ourselves in contested waters?
Perhaps I was really a spy for President Roosevelt...[21]
... and when I was captured, the Japanese forced me to broadcast as "Tokyo Rose."
But my favorite theory claims I married a fisherman...
... and lived to be over 100.
But the truth is...
... I just vanished.
Believe It or Not!

INTO THIN AIR! NOTES

1. Fred Noonan met Amelia sometime in 1937, only a few months before their disappearance. Although Amelia was married to George Putnam, she had attained celebrity status prior to the marriage and still used her maiden name.

2. "Millie" was Amelia's childhood nickname.

3. Lady Lindy was the nickname given to Amelia by Captain H. H. Railey and adopted by the popular press.

4. According to some sources, the last message the Coast Guard cutter *Itasca* received from Amelia was fragmented, but contained the phrases "Cloudy and overcast" and "want bearings."

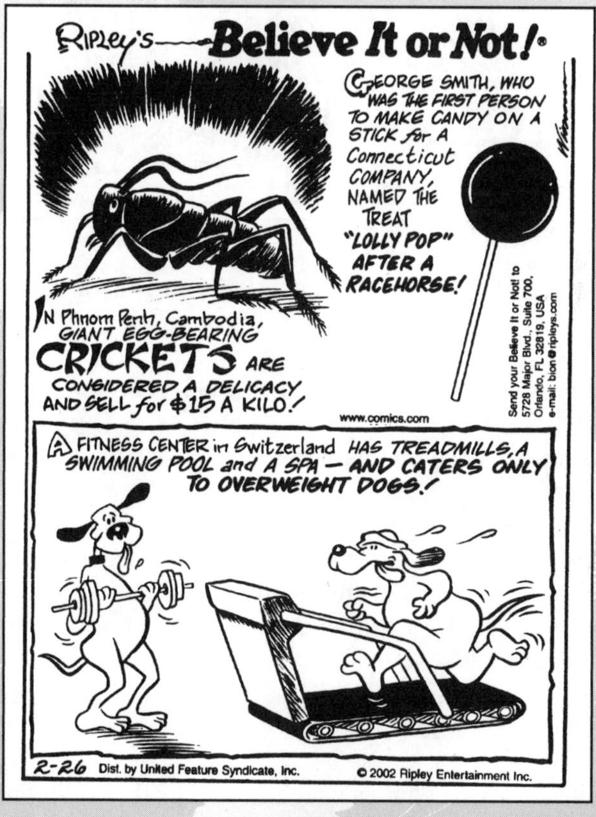

Ripley's Believe It or Not!
GEORGE SMITH, WHO WAS THE FIRST PERSON TO MAKE CANDY ON A STICK for A Connecticut COMPANY, NAMED THE TREAT "LOLLY POP" AFTER A RACEHORSE!
IN Phnom Penh, Cambodia, GIANT EGG-BEARING CRICKETS ARE CONSIDERED A DELICACY AND SELL for $15 A KILO!
www.comics.com
Send your Believe It or Not! to 5728 Major Blvd., Suite 700, Orlando, FL 32819, USA e-mail: bion@ripleys.com
A FITNESS CENTER in Switzerland HAS TREADMILLS, A SWIMMING POOL and A SPA — AND CATERS ONLY TO OVERWEIGHT DOGS!
2-26 Dist. by United Feature Syndicate, Inc.
© 2002 Ripley Entertainment Inc.

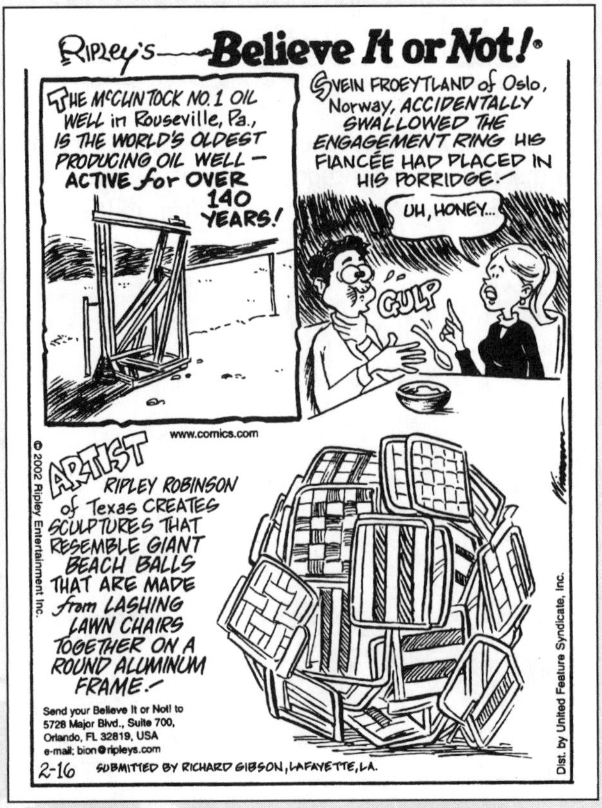
RIPLEY'S Believe It or Not!®
THE McCLINTOCK NO. 1 OIL WELL in Rouseville, Pa., IS THE WORLD'S OLDEST PRODUCING OIL WELL — ACTIVE for OVER 140 YEARS!
SVEIN FROEYTLAND of Oslo, Norway, ACCIDENTALLY SWALLOWED THE ENGAGEMENT RING HIS FIANCÉE HAD PLACED IN HIS PORRIDGE.
UH, HONEY...
GULP
www.comics.com
ARTIST RIPLEY ROBINSON of Texas CREATES SCULPTURES THAT RESEMBLE GIANT BEACH BALLS THAT ARE MADE from LASHING LAWN CHAIRS TOGETHER ON A ROUND ALUMINUM FRAME.
© 2002 Ripley Entertainment Inc.
Send your Believe It or Not! to 5728 Major Blvd., Suite 700, Orlando, FL 32819, USA
e-mail: bion@ripleys.com
2-16
SUBMITTED BY RICHARD GIBSON, LAFAYETTE, LA.
Dist. by United Feature Syndicate, Inc.

5. Or so she told her husband in a letter written shortly before her last flight.

6. Other sources cite this line as Amelia's last known transmission.

7. Most sources place Amelia's birthday as July 24, 1897. She disappeared on July 2, 1937.

8. New York Supreme Court associate justice Joseph. F. Crater vanished on August 6, 1930 after hailing a taxi in the streets of New York. It was one of the most famous disappearances of the time.

9. Roanoke Island was originally part of Virginia. It is now off the coast of North Carolina.

10. Eleanor Dare was White's daughter, and mother of Virginia Dare.

11. Other sources spell it "Croatoan" and also mention another carving, just the word "CRO" in Roman letters.

12. Most sources identify the tribe as Hatteras Indians.

13. Some sources place the number of crewmen at only six.

14. The final fate of the *Mary Celeste*, however, is known. The ship changed hands several times over the next 12 years until she was finally wrecked off of the coast of Haiti as part of an insurance scam. In August 2001, the wreck was located.

15. Well, six, actually.

16. The "D.B." moniker is attributed to a patrolman's error, but has been popularized through the media and a film.

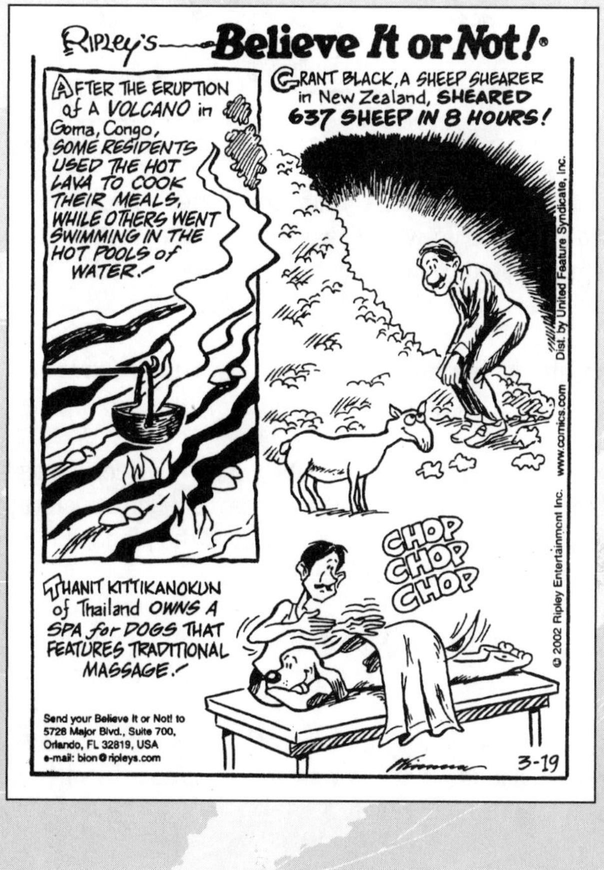

Ripley's Believe It or Not!®
AFTER THE ERUPTION of A VOLCANO in Goma, Congo, SOME RESIDENTS USED THE HOT LAVA TO COOK THEIR MEALS, WHILE OTHERS WENT SWIMMING IN THE HOT POOLS of WATER.
GRANT BLACK, A SHEEP SHEARER in New Zealand, SHEARED 637 SHEEP IN 8 HOURS!
CHOP CHOP CHOP
THANIT KITTIKANOKUN of Thailand OWNS A SPA for DOGS THAT FEATURES TRADITIONAL MASSAGE.
Send your Believe It or Not! to
5728 Major Blvd., Suite 700,
Orlando, FL 32819, USA
e-mail: bion@ripleys.com
3-19
© 2002 Ripley Entertainment Inc. www.comics.com Dist. by United Feature Syndicate, Inc.

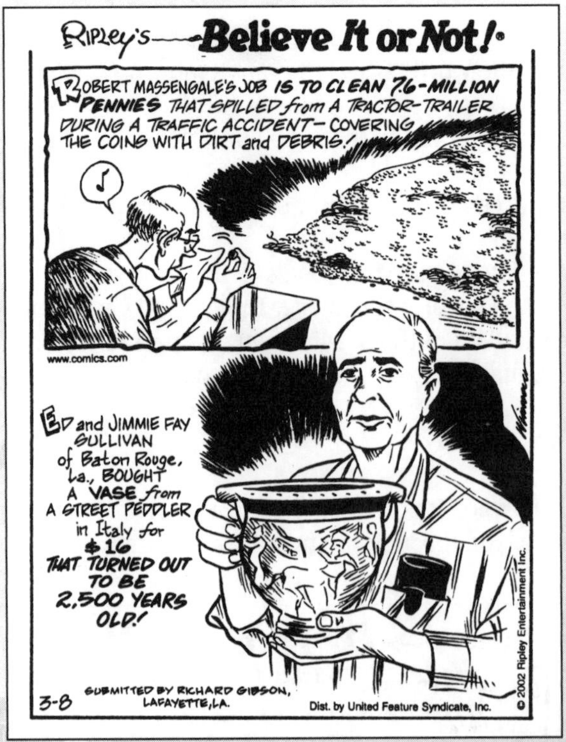
Ripley's Believe It or Not!
ROBERT MASSENGALE'S JOB IS TO CLEAN 7.6-MILLION PENNIES THAT SPILLED from A TRACTOR-TRAILER DURING A TRAFFIC ACCIDENT — COVERING THE COINS WITH DIRT and DEBRIS!
www.comics.com
ED and JIMMIE FAY SULLIVAN of Baton Rouge, La., BOUGHT A VASE from A STREET PEDDLER in Italy for $16 THAT TURNED OUT TO BE 2,500 YEARS OLD!
3-8
SUBMITTED BY RICHARD GIBSON, LAFAYETTE, LA.
Dist. by United Feature Syndicate, Inc.
© 2002 Ripley Entertainment Inc.

17. According to the Naples Daily News (and other sources), Duane Weber confessed to his wife, Jo, while dying of kidney disease in 1995. He was 70. The fact that he used "Dan" rather than the erroneous "D.B." is important, as is his physical resemblance to the skyjacker.

18. According to law enforcement, at least, the case is still open, although many presume Cooper dead.

19. Experts agree that the fuel tanks would have served as flotation devices, provided the landing didn't cause too much structural damage to the plane. A life raft was stowed aboard the plane, but it – like everything else – was never recovered.

20. Roosevelt authorized a search that included nine naval ships and sixty-six aircraft. The search cost over $4 million.

21. Believe it or not, one of the many theories surrounding Amelia's disappearance holds that she was, in fact, gathering intelligence for the President during her flight.

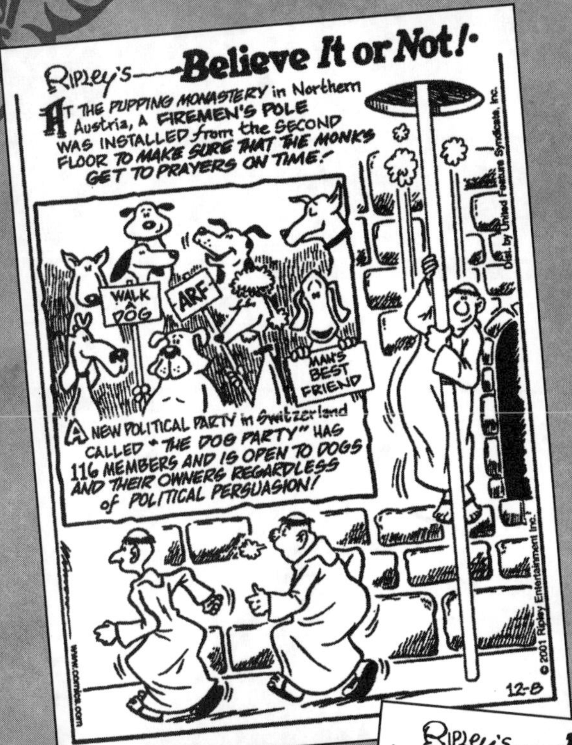
RIPLEY'S Believe It or Not!®
AT THE PUPPING MONASTERY in Northern Austria, A FIREMEN'S POLE WAS INSTALLED from the SECOND FLOOR TO MAKE SURE THAT THE MONKS GET TO PRAYERS ON TIME!
WALK A DOG
ARF
MAN'S BEST FRIEND
A NEW POLITICAL PARTY in Switzerland CALLED "THE DOG PARTY" HAS 116 MEMBERS AND IS OPEN TO DOGS AND THEIR OWNERS REGARDLESS of POLITICAL PERSUASION!
Dist. by United Feature Syndicate, Inc.
© 2001 Ripley Entertainment Inc.
www.comics.com
12-8

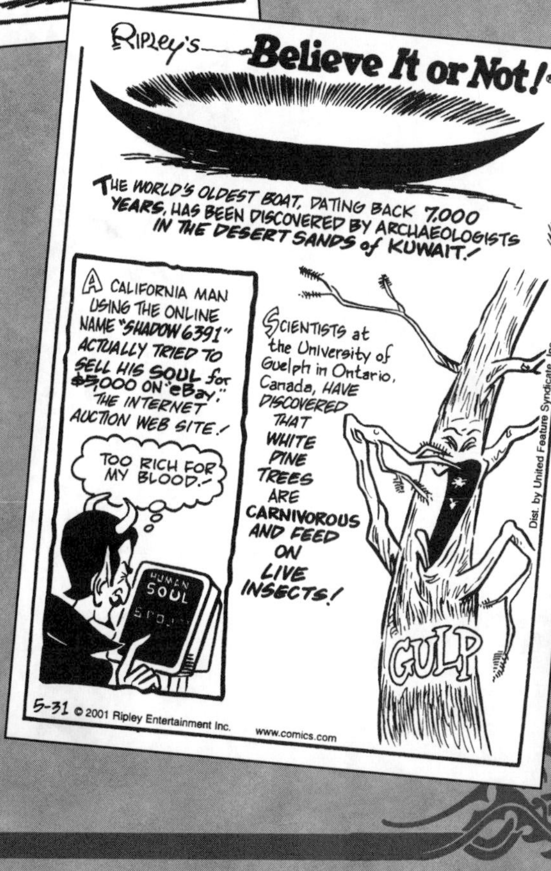
RIPLEY'S Believe It or Not!®
THE WORLD'S OLDEST BOAT, DATING BACK 7,000 YEARS, HAS BEEN DISCOVERED BY ARCHAEOLOGISTS IN THE DESERT SANDS of KUWAIT!
A CALIFORNIA MAN USING THE ONLINE NAME "SHADOW 6391" ACTUALLY TRIED TO SELL HIS SOUL for $5,000 ON "eBay," THE INTERNET AUCTION WEB SITE!
TOO RICH FOR MY BLOOD!
HUMAN SOUL
SCIENTISTS at the University of Guelph in Ontario, Canada, HAVE DISCOVERED THAT WHITE PINE TREES ARE CARNIVOROUS AND FEED ON LIVE INSECTS!
GULP
Dist. by United Feature Syndicate, Inc.
5-31 © 2001 Ripley Entertainment Inc.
www.comics.com

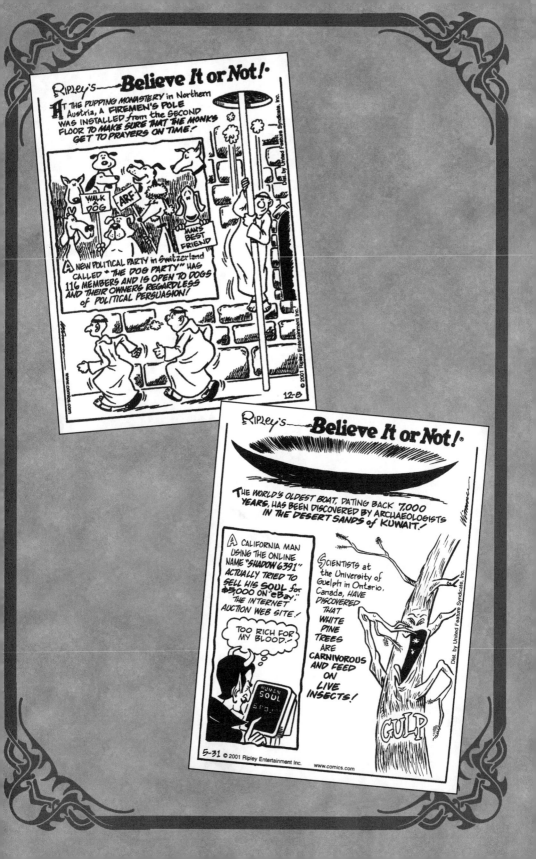

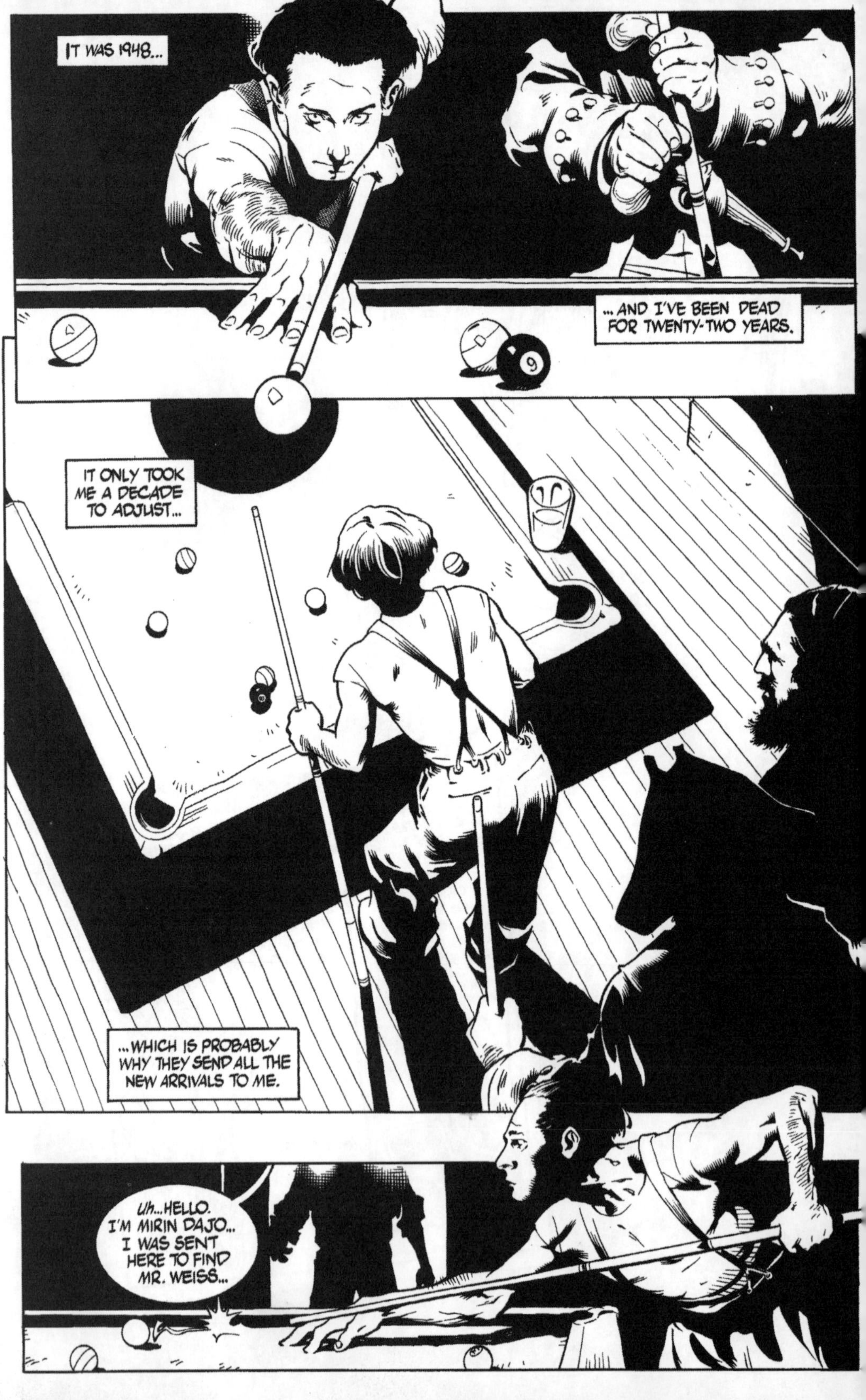
IT WAS 1948...
...AND I'VE BEEN DEAD FOR TWENTY-TWO YEARS.
IT ONLY TOOK ME A DECADE TO ADJUST...
...WHICH IS PROBABLY WHY THEY SEND ALL THE NEW ARRIVALS TO ME.
Uh...HELLO. I'M MIRIN DAJO... I WAS SENT HERE TO FIND MR. WEISS...

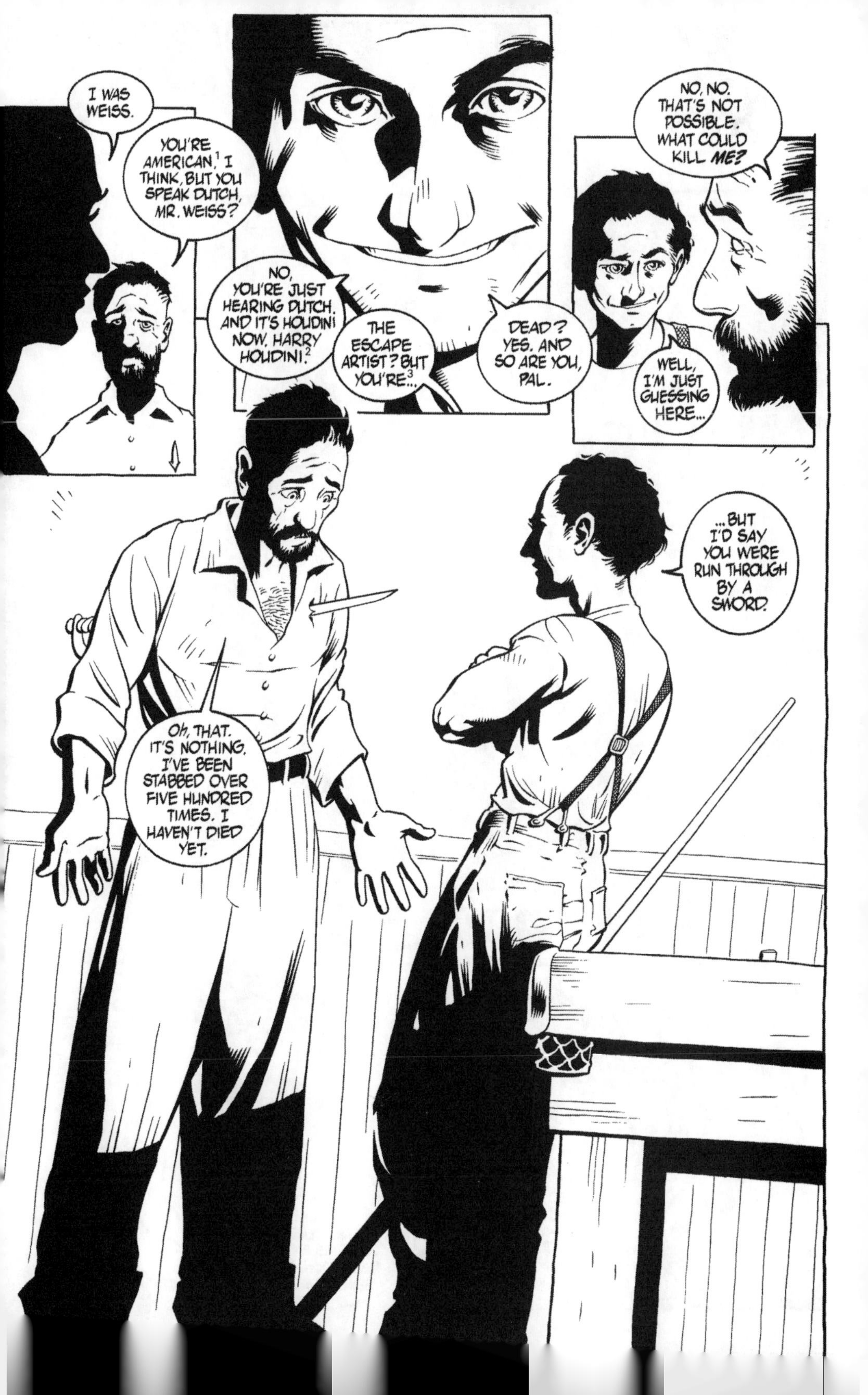
I WAS WEISS.
YOU'RE AMERICAN,[1] I THINK, BUT YOU SPEAK DUTCH, MR. WEISS?
NO, YOU'RE JUST HEARING DUTCH. AND IT'S HOUDINI NOW. HARRY HOUDINI.[2]
THE ESCAPE ARTIST? BUT YOU'RE...[3]
DEAD? YES. AND SO ARE YOU, PAL.
NO, NO. THAT'S NOT POSSIBLE. WHAT COULD KILL *ME?*
WELL, I'M JUST GUESSING HERE...
...BUT I'D SAY YOU WERE RUN THROUGH BY A SWORD.
Oh, THAT. IT'S NOTHING. I'VE BEEN STABBED OVER FIVE HUNDRED TIMES. I HAVEN'T DIED YET.

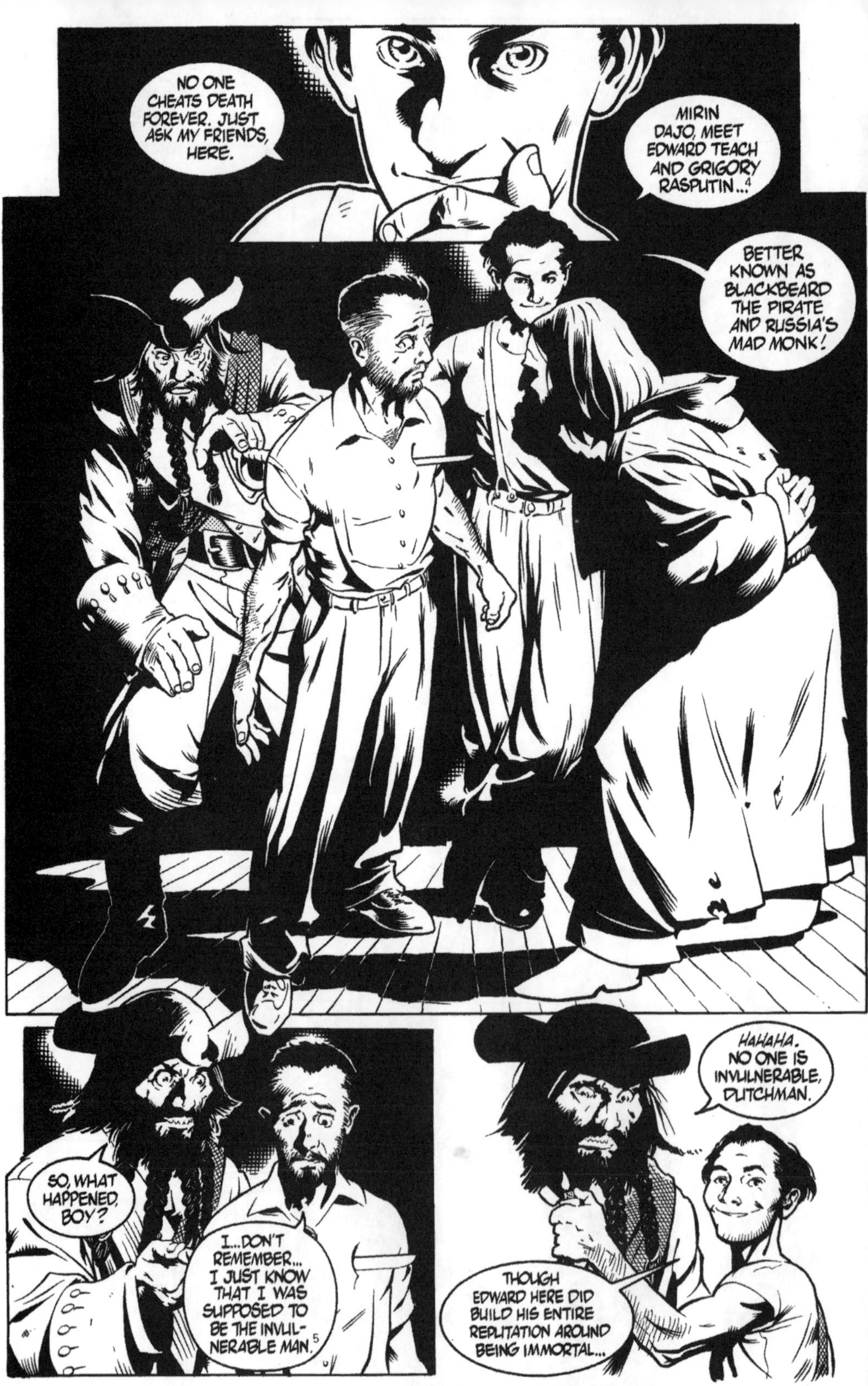
NO ONE CHEATS DEATH FOREVER. JUST ASK MY FRIENDS, HERE.
MIRIN DAJO, MEET EDWARD TEACH AND GRIGORY RASPUTIN...4
BETTER KNOWN AS BLACKBEARD THE PIRATE AND RUSSIA'S MAD MONK!
SO, WHAT HAPPENED, BOY?
I...DON'T REMEMBER... I JUST KNOW THAT I WAS SUPPOSED TO BE THE INVUL-NERABLE MAN.5
HAHAHA. NO ONE IS INVULNERABLE, DUTCHMAN.
THOUGH EDWARD HERE DID BUILD HIS ENTIRE REPUTATION AROUND BEING IMMORTAL...

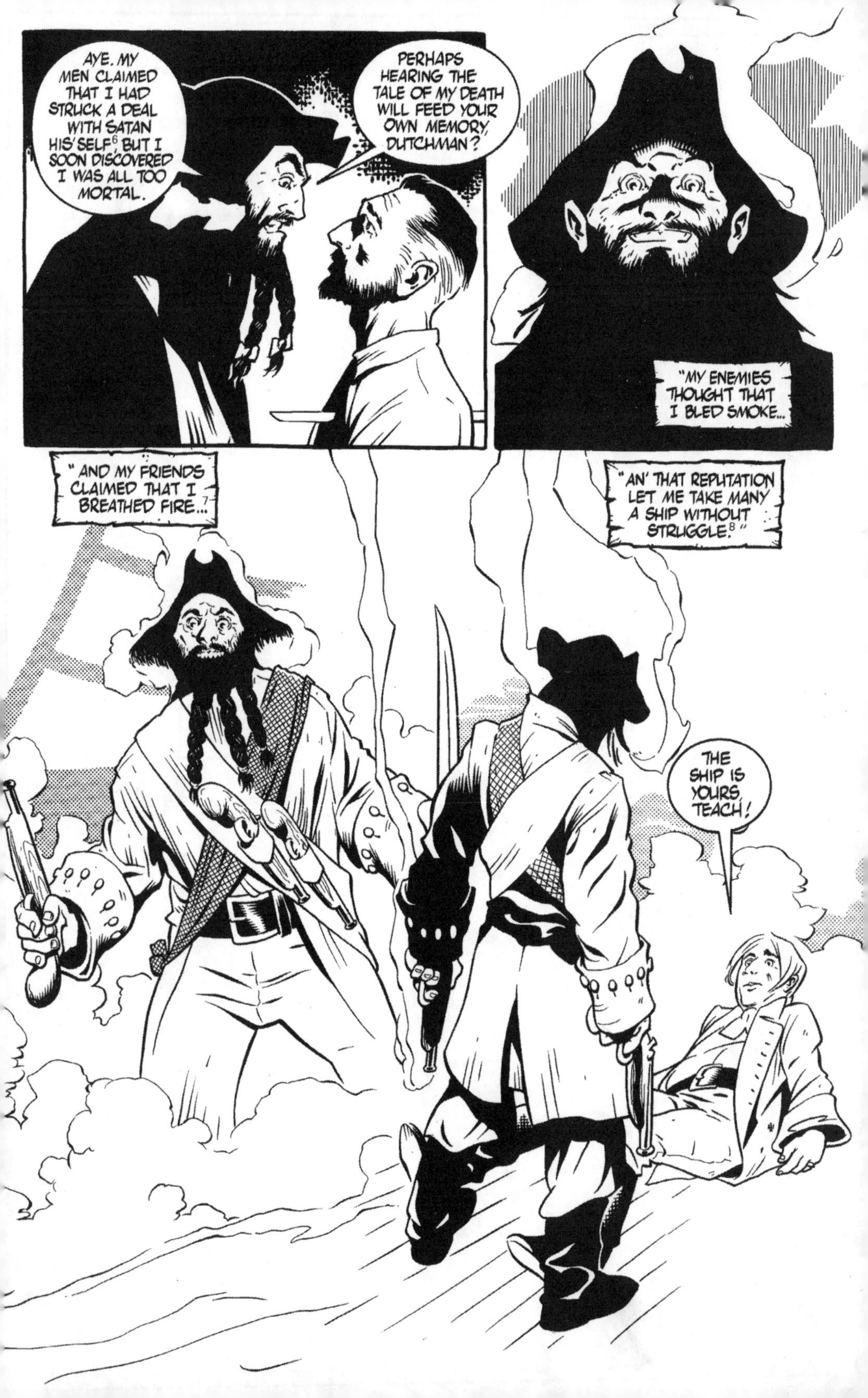
AYE. MY MEN CLAIMED THAT I HAD STRUCK A DEAL WITH SATAN HIS' SELF[6], BUT I SOON DISCOVERED I WAS ALL TOO MORTAL.
PERHAPS HEARING THE TALE OF MY DEATH WILL FEED YOUR OWN MEMORY, DUTCHMAN?
"MY ENEMIES THOUGHT THAT I BLED SMOKE...
"AND MY FRIENDS CLAIMED THAT I BREATHED FIRE...[7]
"AN' THAT REPUTATION LET ME TAKE MANY A SHIP WITHOUT STRUGGLE.[8]"
THE SHIP IS YOURS, TEACH!

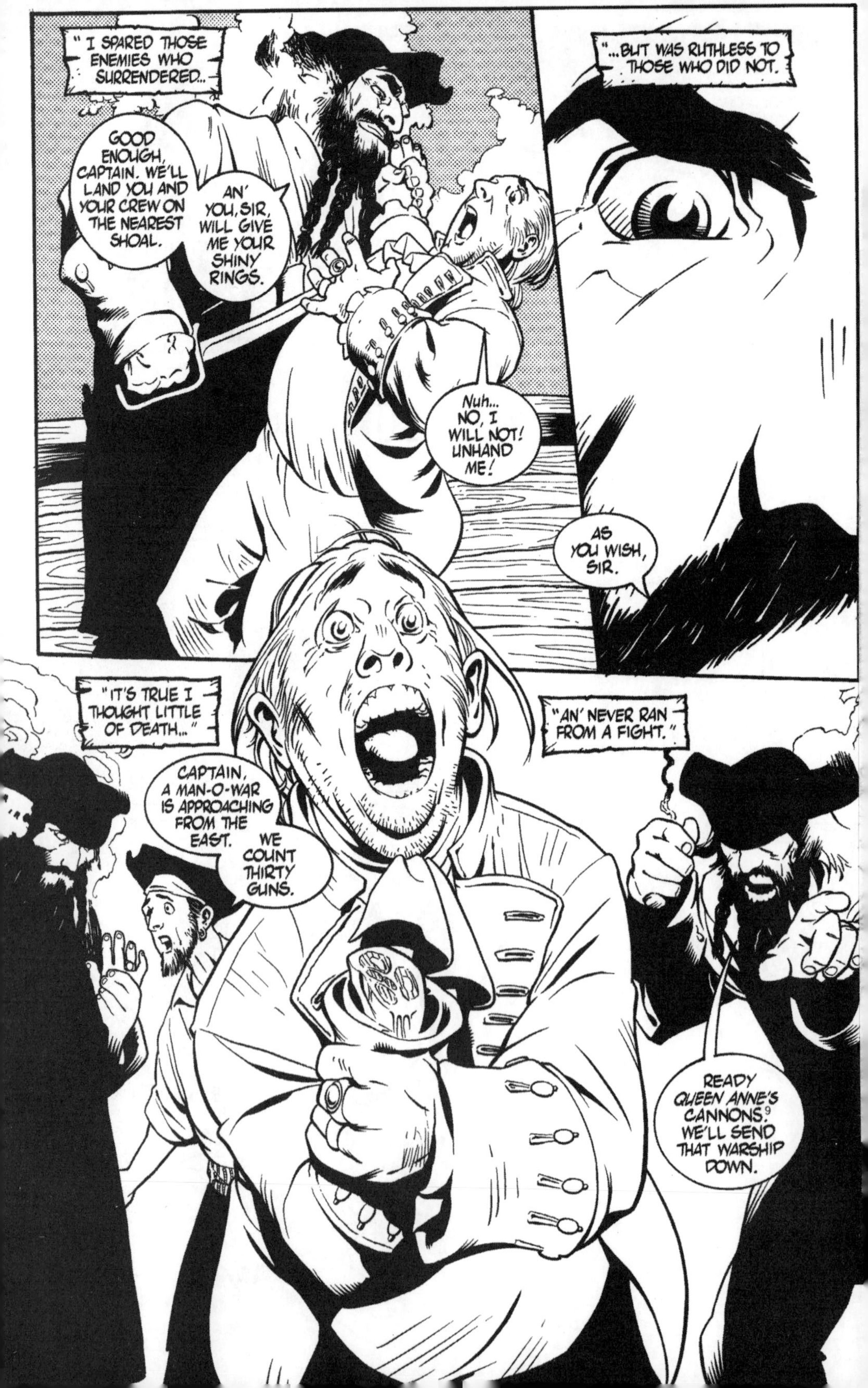
"I SPARED THOSE ENEMIES WHO SURRENDERED...
GOOD ENOUGH, CAPTAIN. WE'LL LAND YOU AND YOUR CREW ON THE NEAREST SHOAL.
AN' YOU, SIR, WILL GIVE ME YOUR SHINY RINGS.
Nuh... NO, I WILL NOT! UNHAND ME!
"...BUT WAS RUTHLESS TO THOSE WHO DID NOT.
AS YOU WISH, SIR.
"IT'S TRUE I THOUGHT LITTLE OF DEATH..."
CAPTAIN, A MAN-O-WAR IS APPROACHING FROM THE EAST.
WE COUNT THIRTY GUNS.
"AN' NEVER RAN FROM A FIGHT."
READY QUEEN ANNE'S CANNONS.[9] WE'LL SEND THAT WARSHIP DOWN.

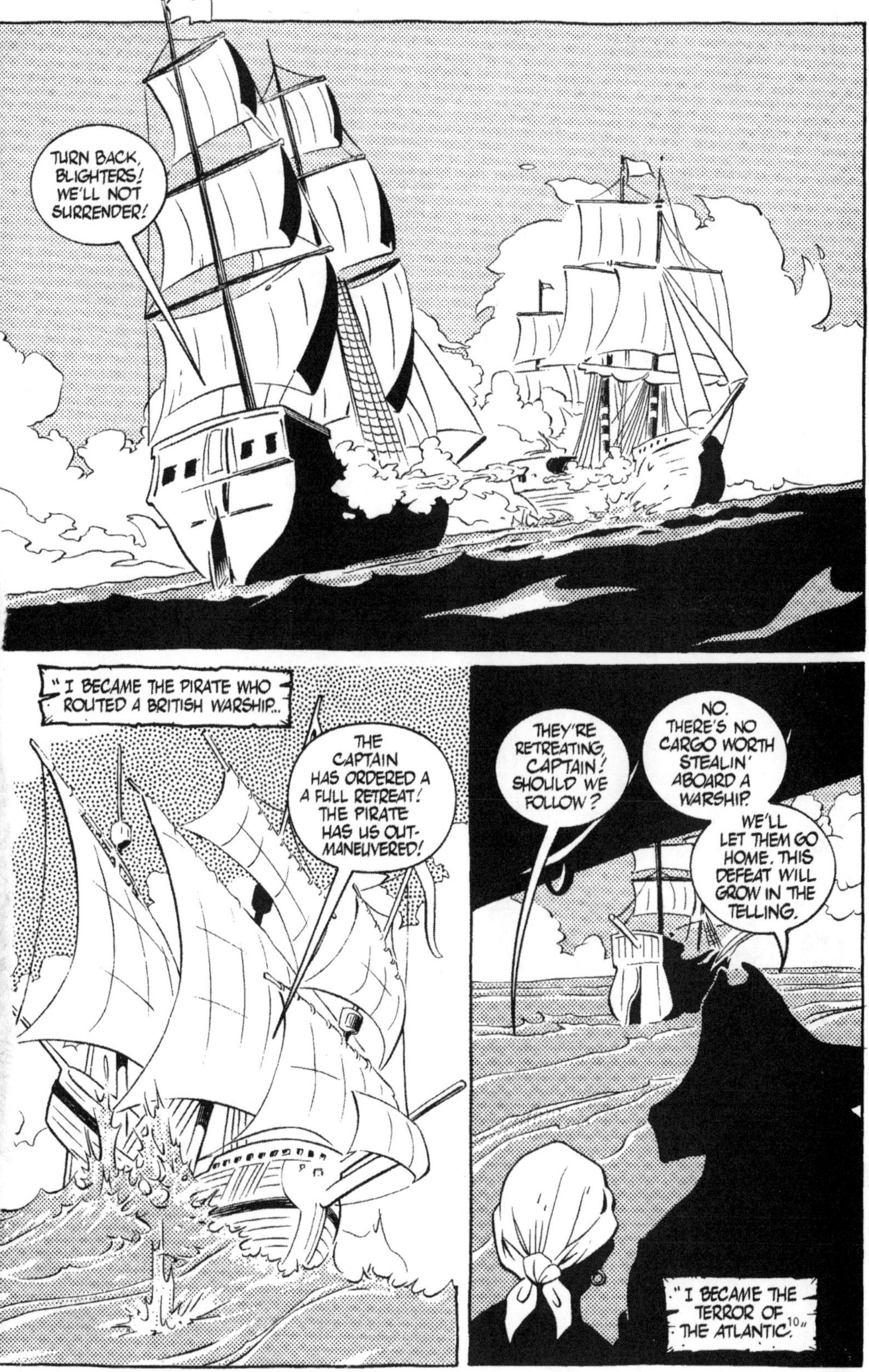
TURN BACK, BLIGHTERS! WE'LL NOT SURRENDER!
"I BECAME THE PIRATE WHO ROUTED A BRITISH WARSHIP...
THE CAPTAIN HAS ORDERED A FULL RETREAT! THE PIRATE HAS US OUT-MANEUVERED!
THEY'RE RETREATING, CAPTAIN! SHOULD WE FOLLOW?
NO. THERE'S NO CARGO WORTH STEALIN' ABOARD A WARSHIP.
WE'LL LET THEM GO HOME. THIS DEFEAT WILL GROW IN THE TELLING.
"I BECAME THE TERROR OF THE ATLANTIC.[10]"

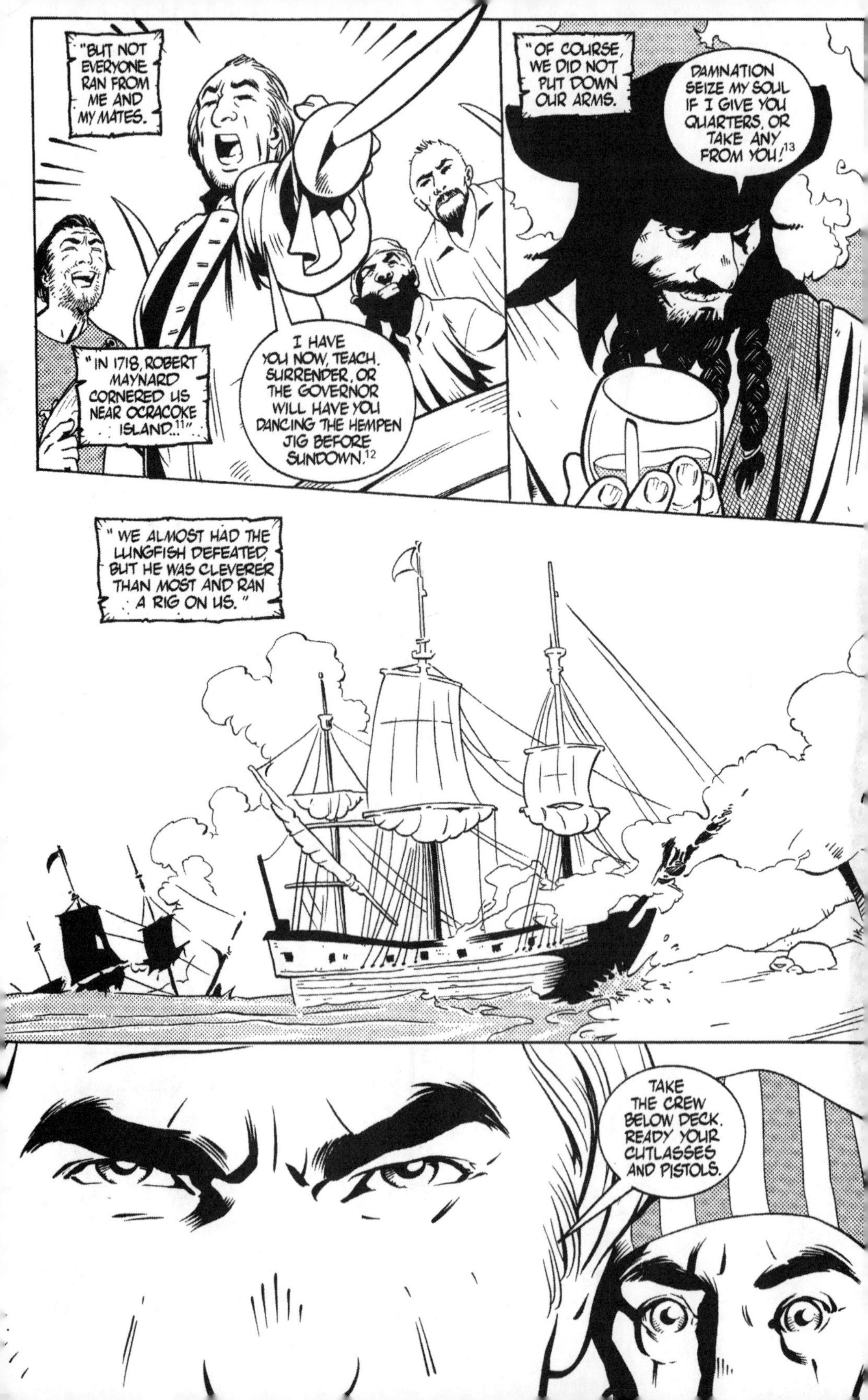
"BUT NOT EVERYONE RAN FROM ME AND MY MATES.
"IN 1718, ROBERT MAYNARD CORNERED US NEAR OCRACOKE ISLAND.[11]"
I HAVE YOU NOW, TEACH. SURRENDER, OR THE GOVERNOR WILL HAVE YOU DANCING THE HEMPEN JIG BEFORE SUNDOWN.[12]
"OF COURSE, WE DID NOT PUT DOWN OUR ARMS.
DAMNATION SEIZE MY SOUL IF I GIVE YOU QUARTERS, OR TAKE ANY FROM YOU![13]
"WE ALMOST HAD THE LUNGFISH DEFEATED, BUT HE WAS CLEVERER THAN MOST AND RAN A RIG ON US."
TAKE THE CREW BELOW DECK. READY YOUR CUTLASSES AND PISTOLS.

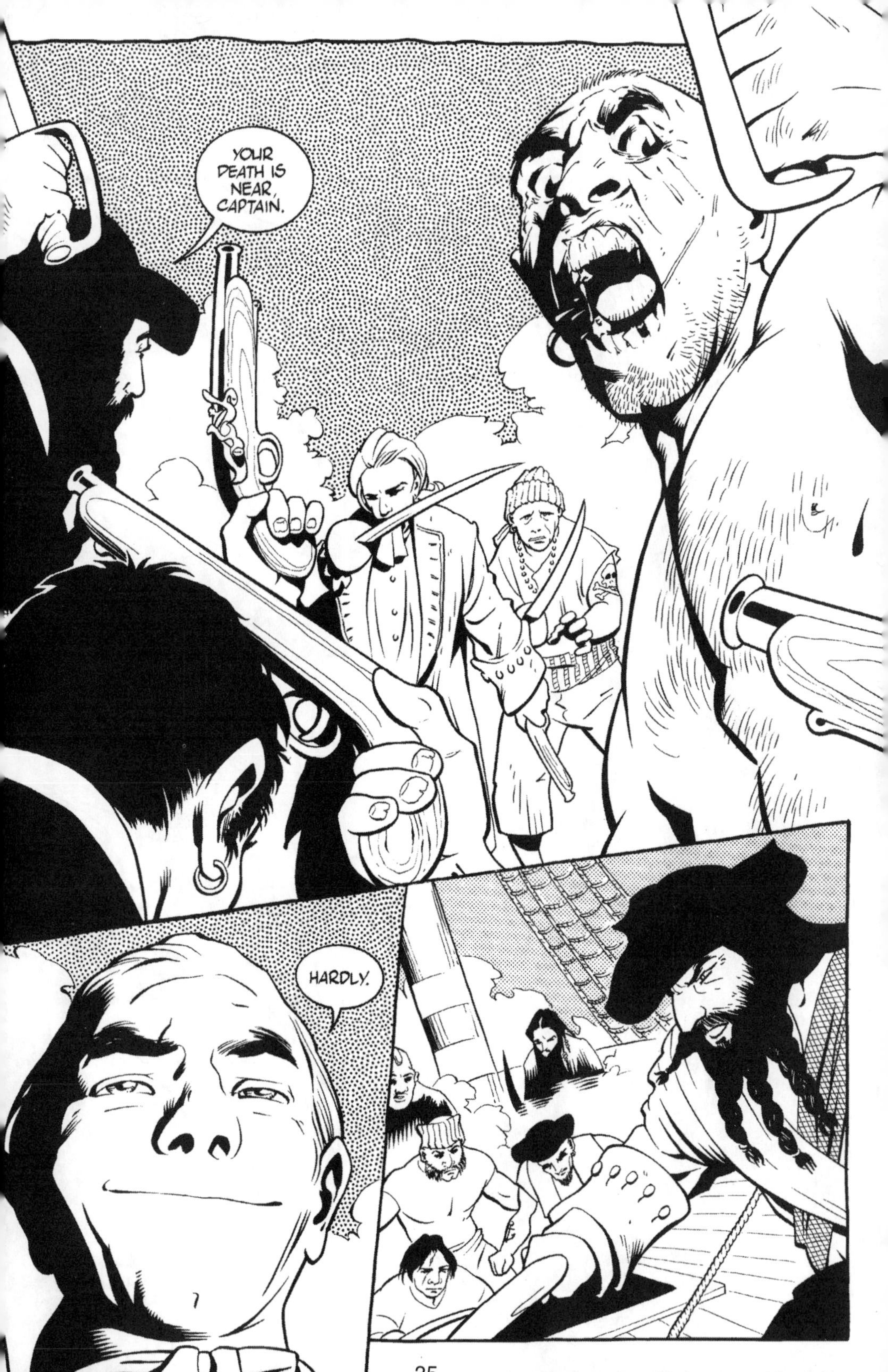
YOUR DEATH IS NEAR, CAPTAIN.
HARDLY.

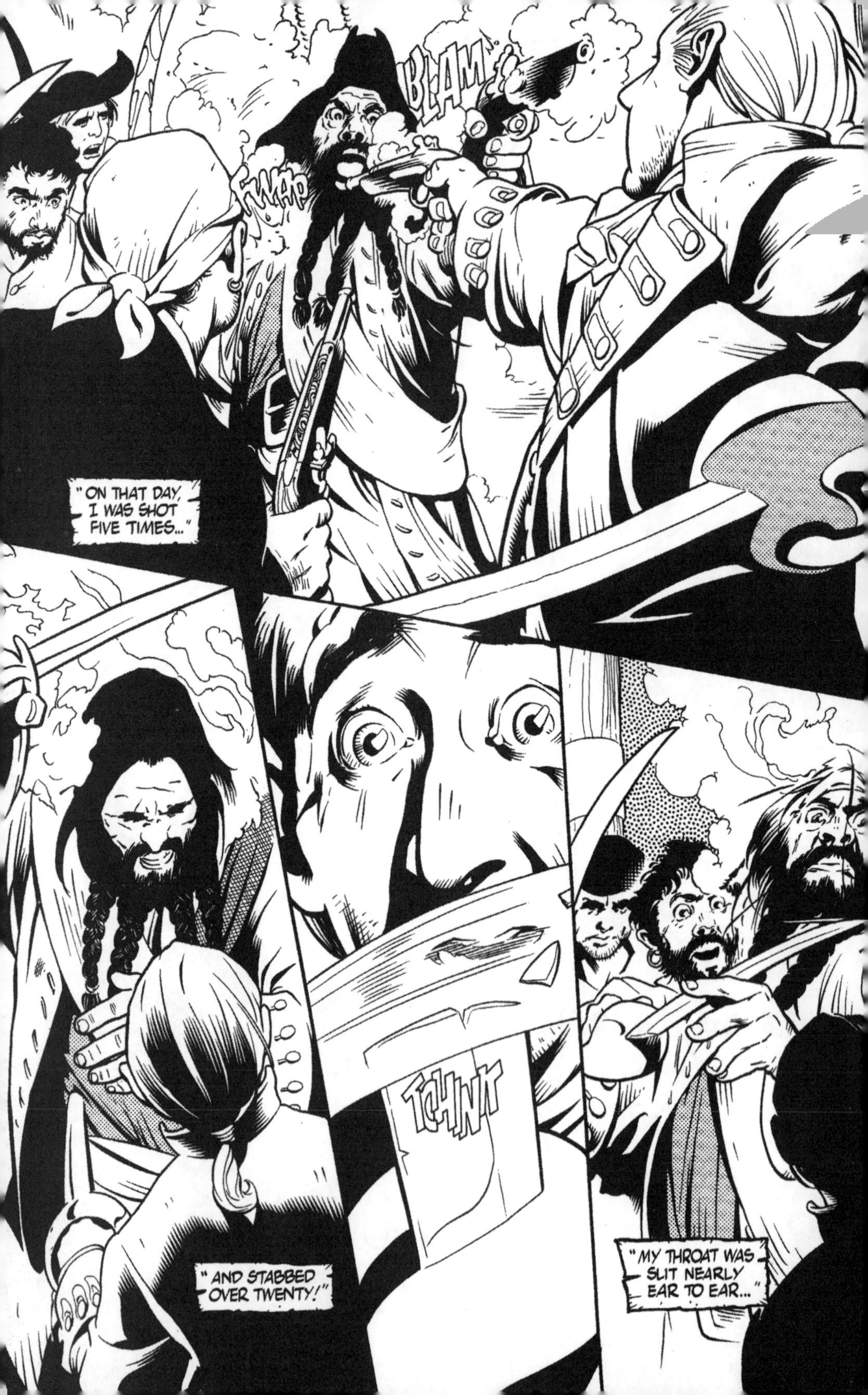
BLAM
FWAP
"ON THAT DAY, I WAS SHOT FIVE TIMES..."
TCHNK
"AND STABBED OVER TWENTY!"
"MY THROAT WAS SLIT NEARLY EAR TO EAR..."

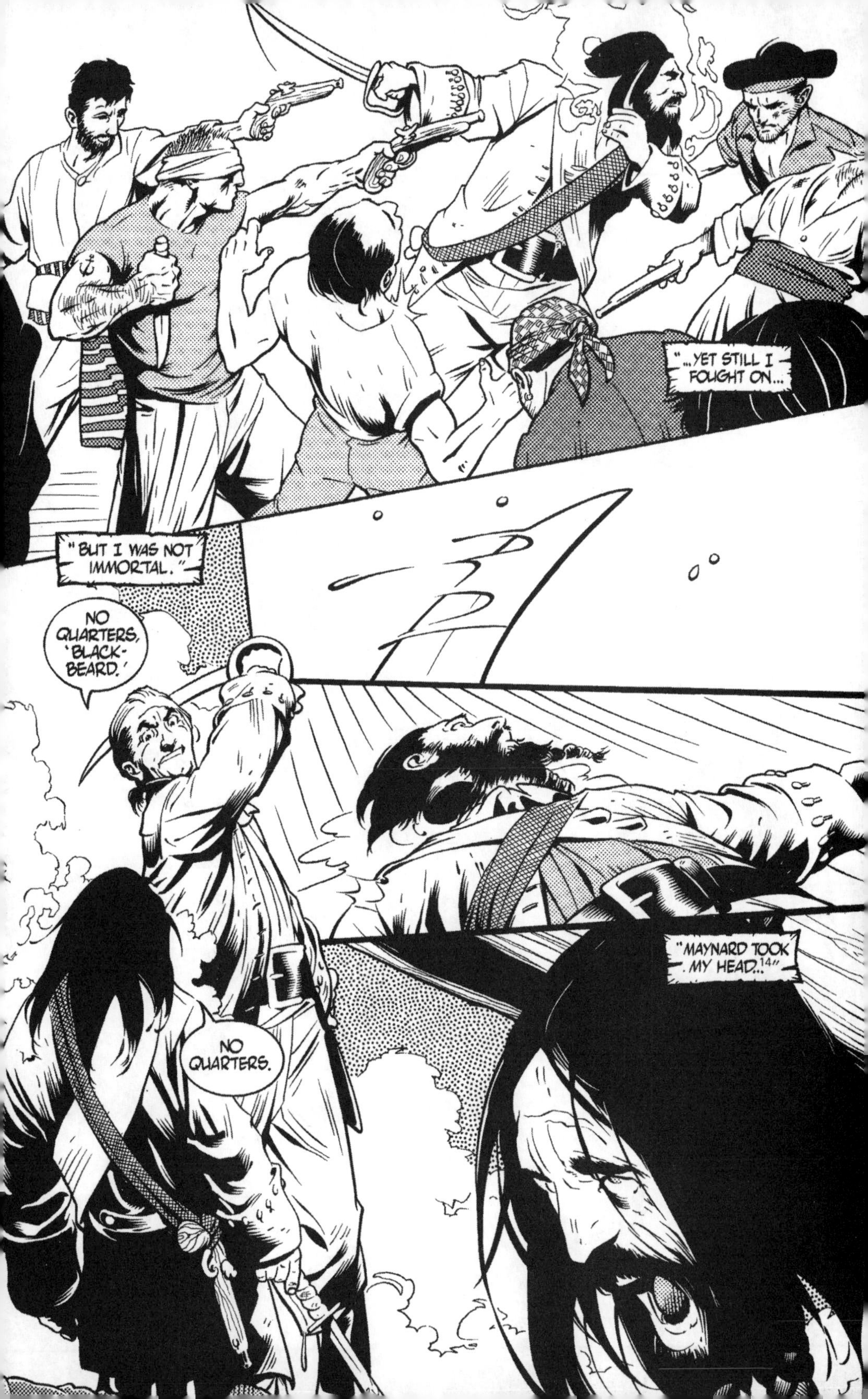
"...YET STILL I FOUGHT ON..."
"BUT I WAS NOT IMMORTAL."
NO QUARTERS, 'BLACK-BEARD.'
"MAYNARD TOOK MY HEAD...14"
NO QUARTERS.

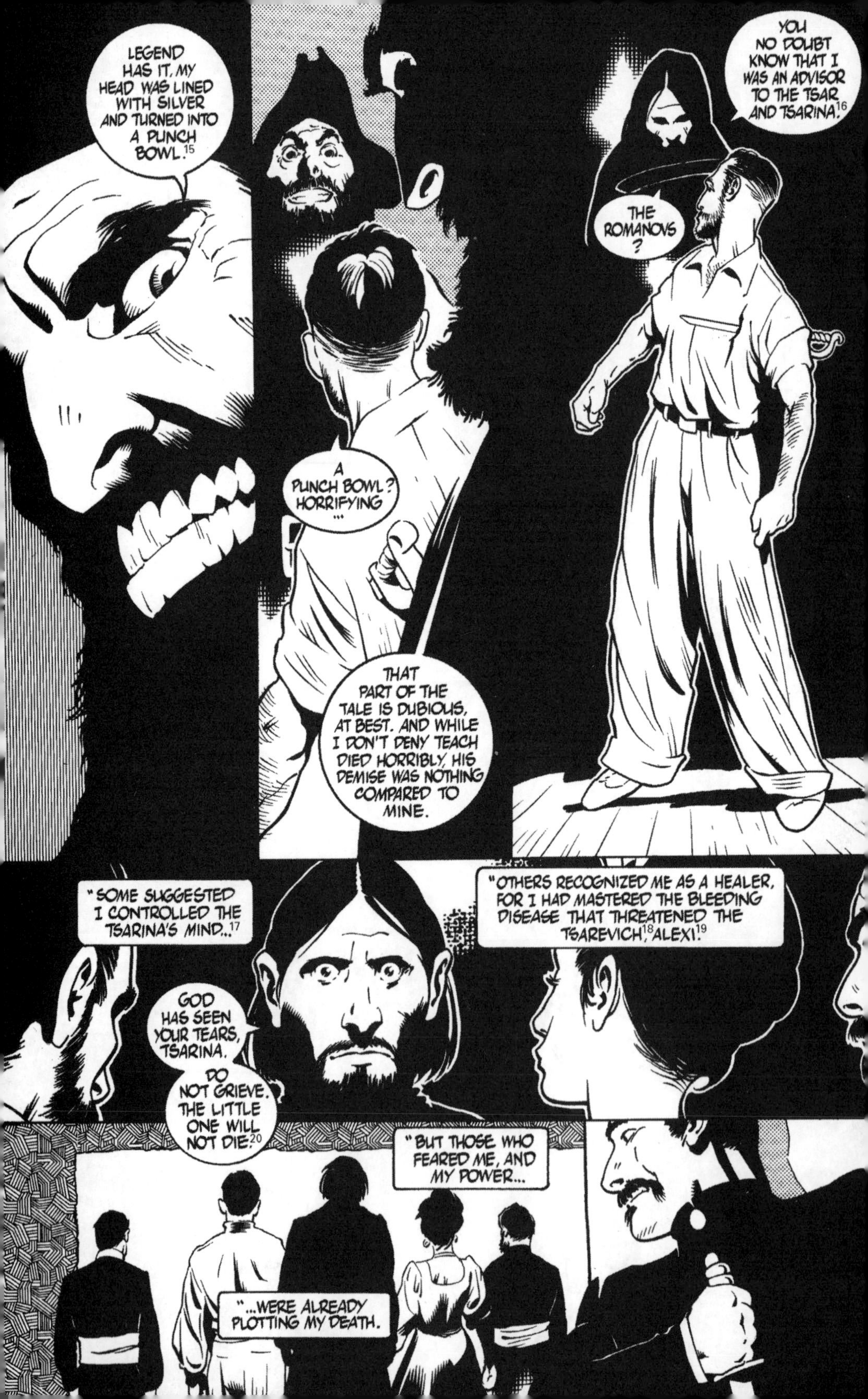
LEGEND HAS IT, MY HEAD WAS LINED WITH SILVER AND TURNED INTO A PUNCH BOWL.[15]
A PUNCH BOWL? HORRIFYING...
THAT PART OF THE TALE IS DUBIOUS, AT BEST. AND WHILE I DON'T DENY TEACH DIED HORRIBLY, HIS DEMISE WAS NOTHING COMPARED TO MINE.
YOU NO DOUBT KNOW THAT I WAS AN ADVISOR TO THE TSAR AND TSARINA.[16]
THE ROMANOVS?
"SOME SUGGESTED I CONTROLLED THE TSARINA'S MIND...[17]
"OTHERS RECOGNIZED ME AS A HEALER, FOR I HAD MASTERED THE BLEEDING DISEASE THAT THREATENED THE TSAREVICH,[18] ALEXI.[19]
GOD HAS SEEN YOUR TEARS, TSARINA.
DO NOT GRIEVE. THE LITTLE ONE WILL NOT DIE.[20]
"BUT THOSE WHO FEARED ME, AND MY POWER...
"...WERE ALREADY PLOTTING MY DEATH.

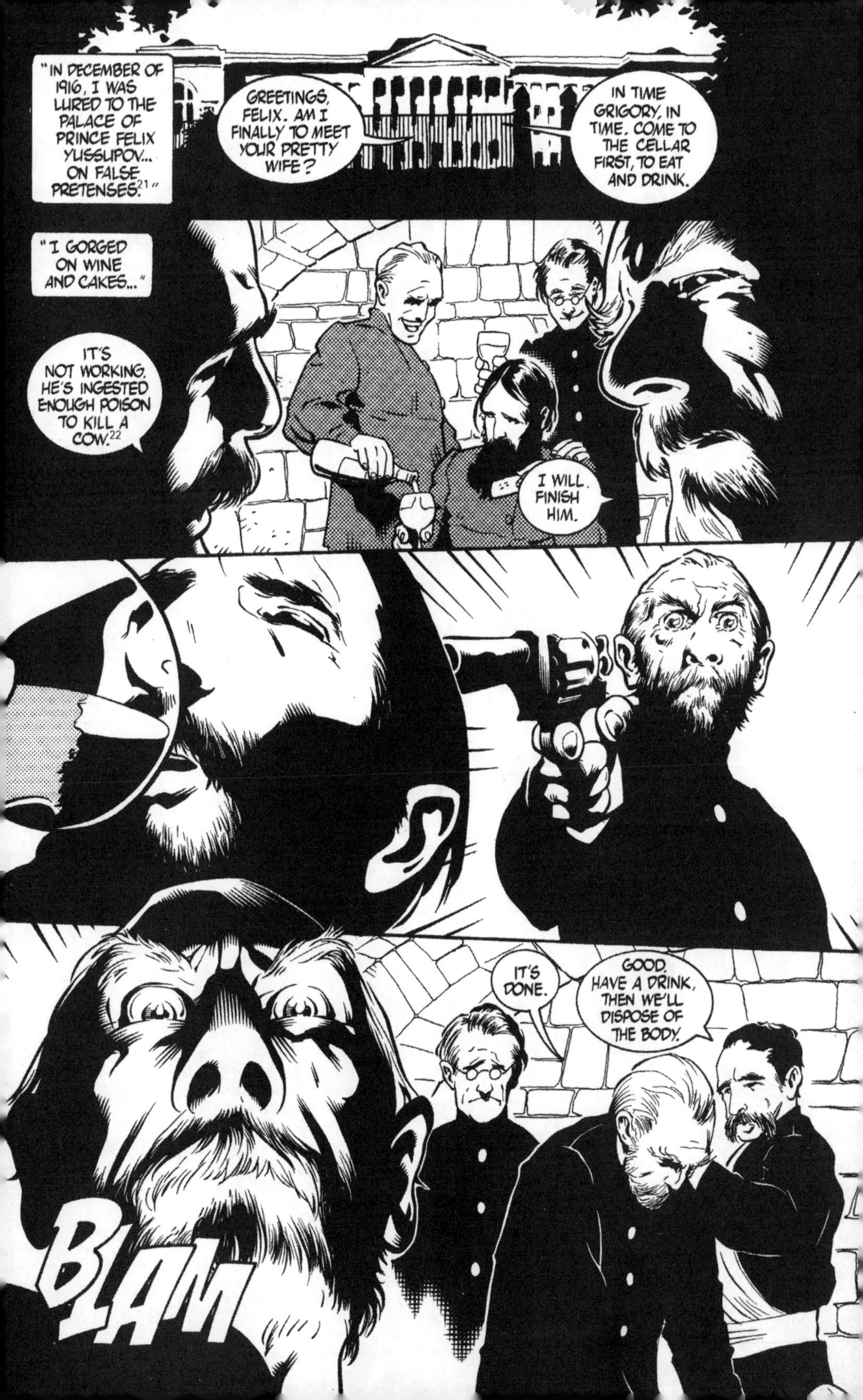
"IN DECEMBER OF 1916, I WAS LURED TO THE PALACE OF PRINCE FELIX YUSSUPOV... ON FALSE PRETENSES.[21]"
GREETINGS, FELIX. AM I FINALLY TO MEET YOUR PRETTY WIFE?
IN TIME GRIGORY, IN TIME. COME TO THE CELLAR FIRST, TO EAT AND DRINK.
"I GORGED ON WINE AND CAKES..."
IT'S NOT WORKING. HE'S INGESTED ENOUGH POISON TO KILL A COW.[22]
I WILL. FINISH HIM.
BLAM
IT'S DONE.
GOOD. HAVE A DRINK, THEN WE'LL DISPOSE OF THE BODY.

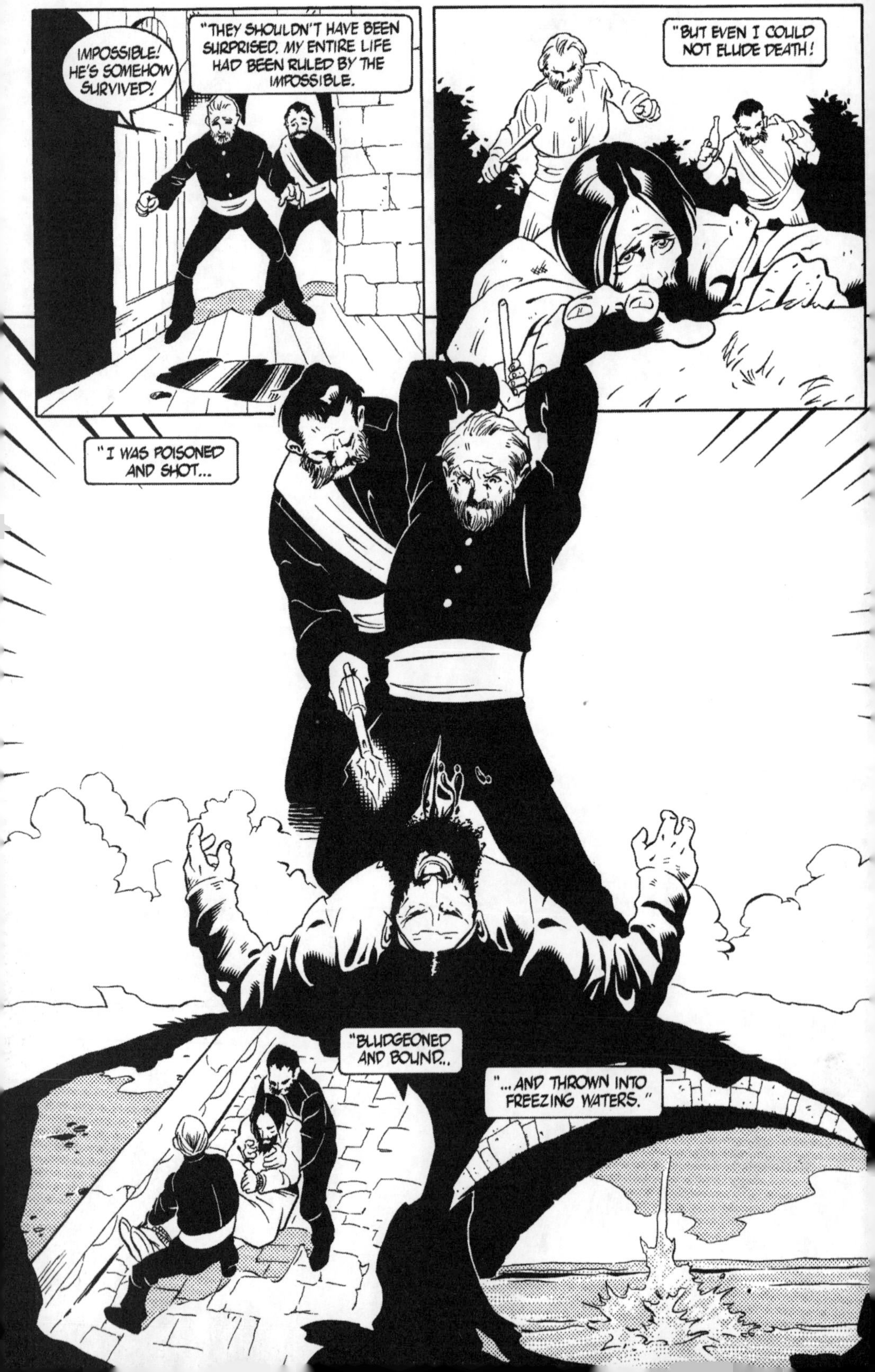
IMPOSSIBLE! HE'S SOMEHOW SURVIVED!
"THEY SHOULDN'T HAVE BEEN SURPRISED. MY ENTIRE LIFE HAD BEEN RULED BY THE IMPOSSIBLE.
"BUT EVEN I COULD NOT ELUDE DEATH!
"I WAS POISONED AND SHOT...
"BLUDGEONED AND BOUND...
"...AND THROWN INTO FREEZING WATERS."

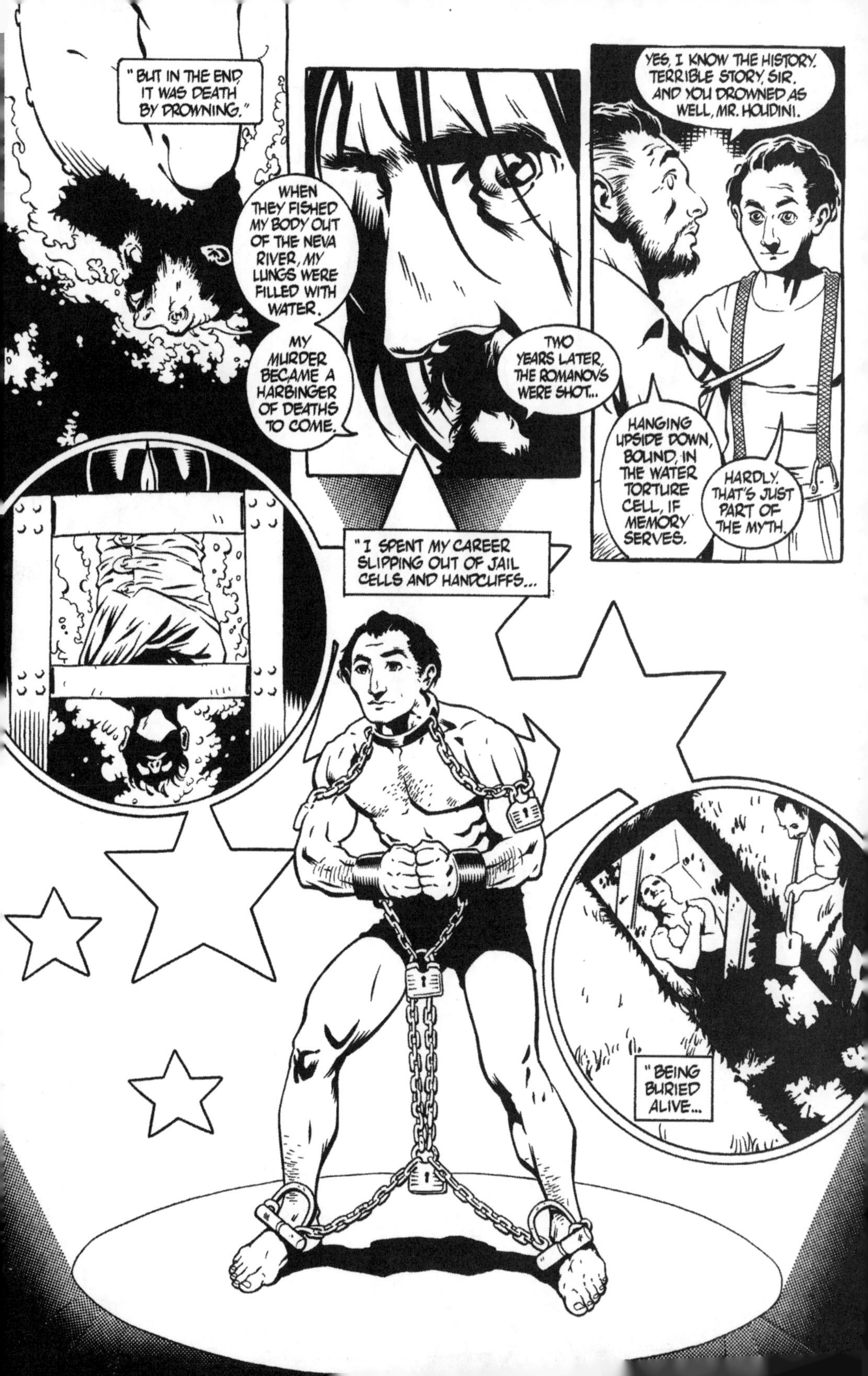
"BUT IN THE END IT WAS DEATH BY DROWNING."
WHEN THEY FISHED MY BODY OUT OF THE NEVA RIVER, MY LUNGS WERE FILLED WITH WATER.
MY MURDER BECAME A HARBINGER OF DEATHS TO COME.
TWO YEARS LATER, THE ROMANOVS WERE SHOT...
YES, I KNOW THE HISTORY. TERRIBLE STORY, SIR. AND YOU DROWNED AS WELL, MR. HOUDINI.
HANGING UPSIDE DOWN, BOUND, IN THE WATER TORTURE CELL, IF MEMORY SERVES.
HARDLY. THAT'S JUST PART OF THE MYTH.
"I SPENT MY CAREER SLIPPING OUT OF JAIL CELLS AND HANDCUFFS...
"BEING BURIED ALIVE...

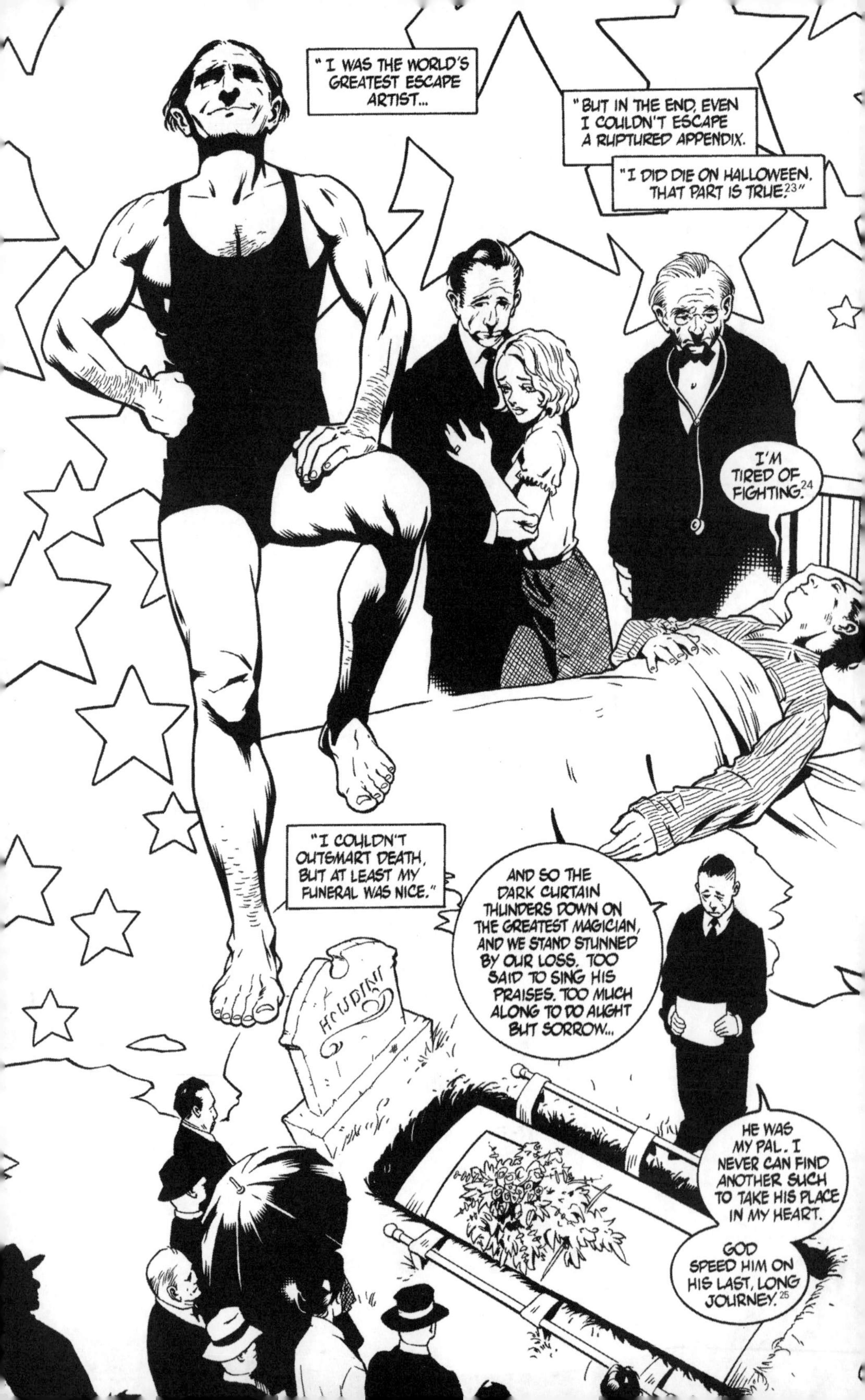
"I WAS THE WORLD'S GREATEST ESCAPE ARTIST...
"BUT IN THE END, EVEN I COULDN'T ESCAPE A RUPTURED APPENDIX.
"I DID DIE ON HALLOWEEN. THAT PART IS TRUE.[23]"
I'M TIRED OF FIGHTING.[24]
"I COULDN'T OUTSMART DEATH, BUT AT LEAST MY FUNERAL WAS NICE."
AND SO THE DARK CURTAIN THUNDERS DOWN ON THE GREATEST MAGICIAN, AND WE STAND STUNNED BY OUR LOSS. TOO SAID TO SING HIS PRAISES. TOO MUCH ALONG TO DO AUGHT BUT SORROW...
HOUDINI
HE WAS MY PAL. I NEVER CAN FIND ANOTHER SUCH TO TAKE HIS PLACE IN MY HEART.
GOD SPEED HIM ON HIS LAST, LONG JOURNEY.[25]

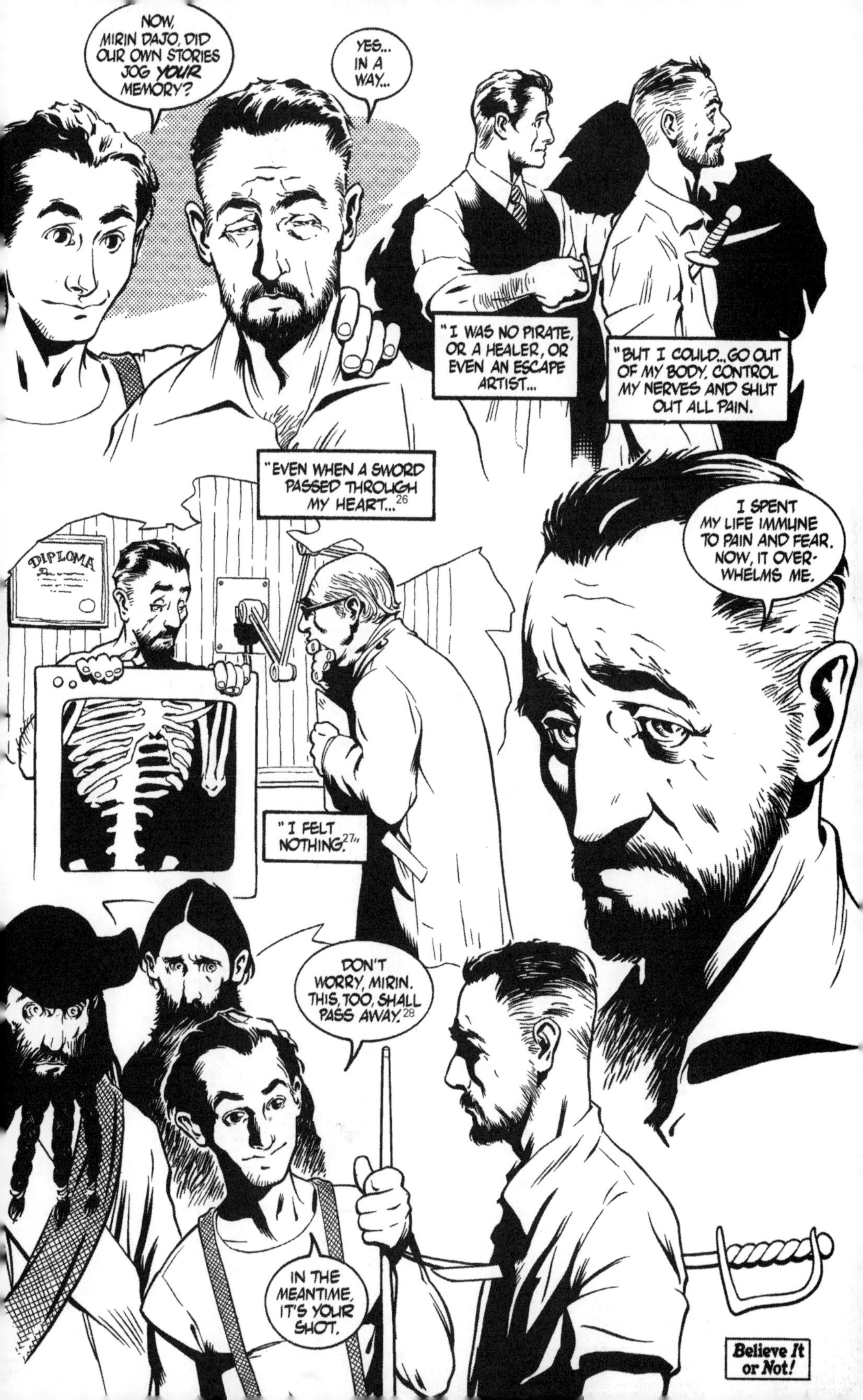
NOW, MIRIN DAJO, DID OUR OWN STORIES JOG YOUR MEMORY?
YES... IN A WAY...
"I WAS NO PIRATE, OR A HEALER, OR EVEN AN ESCAPE ARTIST...
"BUT I COULD...GO OUT OF MY BODY, CONTROL MY NERVES AND SHUT OUT ALL PAIN.
"EVEN WHEN A SWORD PASSED THROUGH MY HEART...[26]
DIPLOMA
"I FELT NOTHING.[27]"
I SPENT MY LIFE IMMUNE TO PAIN AND FEAR. NOW, IT OVER-WHELMS ME.
DON'T WORRY, MIRIN. THIS, TOO, SHALL PASS AWAY.[28]
IN THE MEANTIME, IT'S YOUR SHOT.
Believe It or Not!

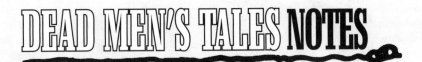

DEAD MEN'S TALES NOTES

1. Although Houdini always claimed that he was born in Wisconsin, he was actually born in Budapest, Hungary. His family moved to the United States when Houdini was four.

2. Harry Houdini's given name was Erich Weiss.

3. Given his chosen profession, it's likely that Mirin Dajo would have known of Houdini, who remains one of the most famous showmen of all time.

4. Interestingly, it is believed that all four figures in this story had assumed names. Mirin Dajo was born Henske Arnold Gerit, while, as we've already discovered, Houdini's given name was Erich Weiss. "Edward Teach" is believed a false identity used by Blackbeard the pirate to protect the reputation of any family in England. Other surnames attributed to Blackbeard include Drummond, Tash, and Thatch. The validity of Rasputin's name, usually cited as "Grigory Yefimovich Rasputin" has also been called into question.

5. The "invulnerable man" was, in fact, Dajo's nickname. His stage name "Mirin Dajo" allegedly means "Something Wonderful" in Esperanto.

6. Among the many legends surrounding Blackbeard, one claims that he often had Satan as a guest on his ship. Other stories asserted that Blackbeard was, in fact, Satan in human guise.

Ripley's Believe It or Not!®
Believe It or Not!
FIVE MILLION BACTERIA CAN LIVE ON A SINGLE .155 SQ. INCH of the HUMAN BODY!
SUBMITTED BY RICHARD GIBSON, LAFAYETTE, LA.
IN HOT SPRINGS, ARK., A RAIN of DEAD DUCKS FELL from the SKY AFTER A THUNDERSTORM!
SCATTERED MALLARDS...
ARKANSAS
www.comics.com
ALAN RICHARD ALCOTT of Derbyshire, England, HAS A COLLECTION of 504 BAR TOWELS from PUBS ALL OVER THE WORLD!
Bob's PUB
MICKEY O's
O'CONNOR'S
3-14
Dist. by United Feature Syndicate, Inc.
© 2002 Ripley Entertainment Inc.

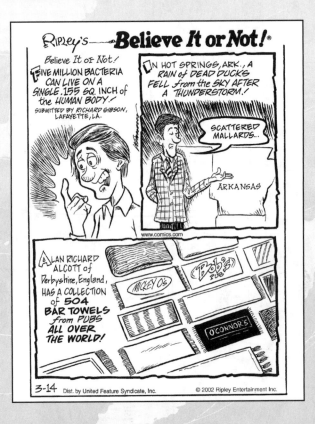

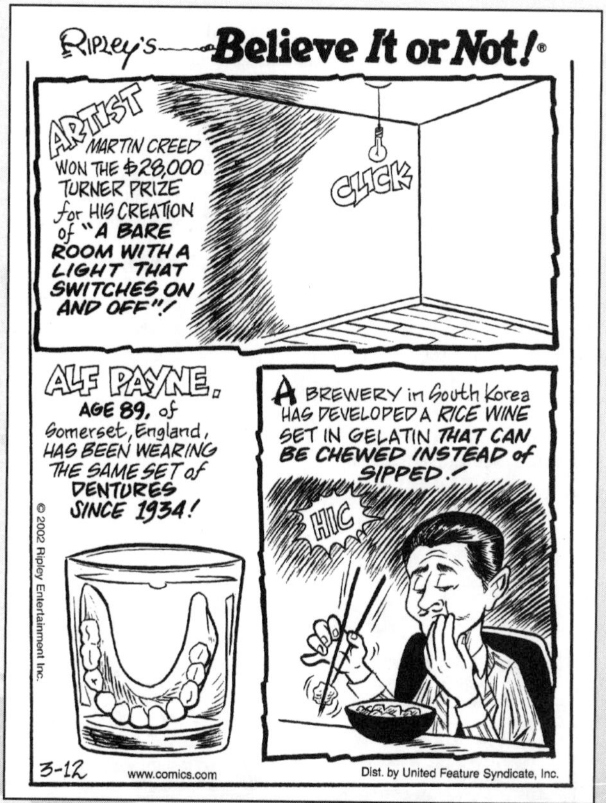
Ripley's Believe It or Not!
ARTIST MARTIN CREED WON THE $28,000 TURNER PRIZE for HIS CREATION of "A BARE ROOM WITH A LIGHT THAT SWITCHES ON AND OFF"!
CLICK
ALF PAYNE, AGE 89, of Somerset, England, HAS BEEN WEARING THE SAME SET of DENTURES SINCE 1934!
A BREWERY in South Korea HAS DEVELOPED A RICE WINE SET IN GELATIN THAT CAN BE CHEWED INSTEAD of SIPPED!
HIC
© 2002 Ripley Entertainment Inc.
3-12
www.comics.com
Dist. by United Feature Syndicate, Inc.

7. Blackbeard allegedly tied cannon fuses into his beard in order to create the illusion that he was surrounded by smoke. He was also known to lace his drinks with gunpowder to allow him to "breath fire" by spitting the liquid through a candle's flame.

8. Blackbeard was not the most accomplished pirate. He captured very few vessels of any worth during his fifteen months of piracy. However, of those ships he did capture, many were taken with minimal bloodshed due to the pirate's fearsome reputation.

9. The full name of Blackbeard's ship was the *Queen Anne's Revenge*.

10. Teach and his crew did, in fact, force the retreat of the British warship *HMS Scarborough* early in the pirate's career. This engagement probably did more to secure Blackbeard's reputation than any of his subsequent raids.

11. Ocracoke Island, off the coast of North Carolina.

12. The "governor" in this case was Governor Alexander Spotswood of Virginia, who hired Maynard to track down and capture Blackbeard. Some researchers believe that Spotswood commissioned (and personally funded) the search for Blackbeard because he hoped to recover the pirate's treasure for himself.

13. According to journalist and author Daniel Defoe, who did more than anyone to grow the legend of Blackbeard, this was the pirate's "toast" to Maynard before they began their epic battle.

14. As depicted here, all details of Blackbeard's death are "true," at least as reported at the time. Blackbeard had successfully disabled one sloop and wounded the second when Maynard sent his crew below decks to goad Blackbeard into boarding. When the pirate captain did board, he and his small crew of less than two dozen were quickly overwhelmed. By all accounts, Blackbeard fought ferociously. Cause of death was identified as decapitation, but he had received five gunshot wounds and at least twenty life-threatening stab wounds, along with the terrible throat-slashing.

15. Many legends surround Blackbeard, including one about the fate of his head; according to some sources, Blackbeard's oversized head was purchased by a plantation owner who turned it into a silver-plated punch bowl. The fate of the punch bowl – if it ever existed – remains unknown.

16. Around 1911, Rasputin became one of Tsar Nicholas II's advisors.

17. The degree to which Rasputin actually influenced the Tsar and Tsarina remains open to debate. At the far end of the spectrum, some researchers believe that Rasputin could mesmerize others with his uncanny eyes.

18. Heir to the throne.

19. Rasputin allegedly had a strange ability to control Alexei's hemophilia, perhaps by putting the boy into meditative trances.

20. This line is actually a sentiment that Rasputin conveyed to the Tsarina via a telegram to the Tsarina after Alexei suffered a dangerous fall.

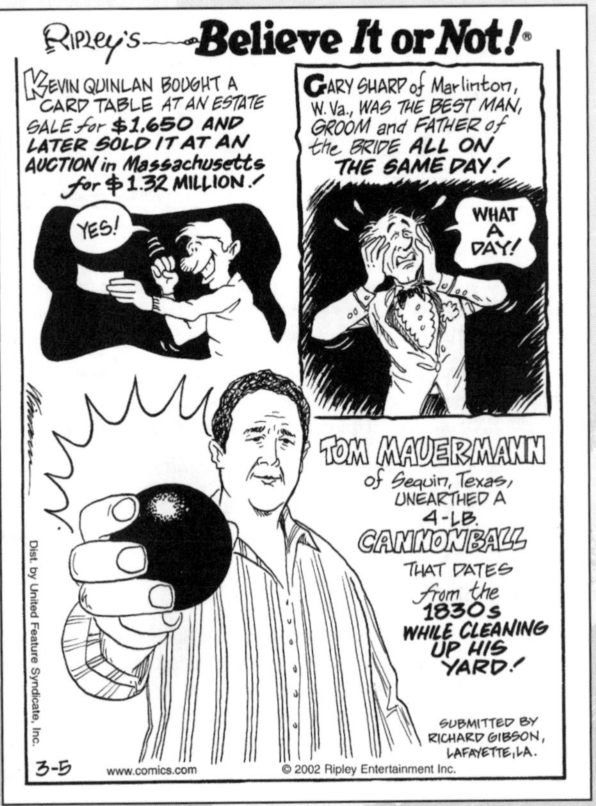
Ripley's Believe It or Not!®
KEVIN QUINLAN BOUGHT A CARD TABLE AT AN ESTATE SALE for $1,650 AND LATER SOLD IT AT AN AUCTION in Massachusetts for $1.32 MILLION!
YES!
GARY SHARP of Marlinton, W. Va., WAS THE BEST MAN, GROOM and FATHER of the BRIDE ALL ON THE SAME DAY!
WHAT A DAY!
TOM MAUERMANN of Sequin, Texas, UNEARTHED A 4-LB. CANNONBALL THAT DATES from the 1830s WHILE CLEANING UP HIS YARD!
SUBMITTED BY RICHARD GIBSON, LAFAYETTE, LA.
Dist. by United Feature Syndicate, Inc.
3-5
www.comics.com
© 2002 Ripley Entertainment Inc.

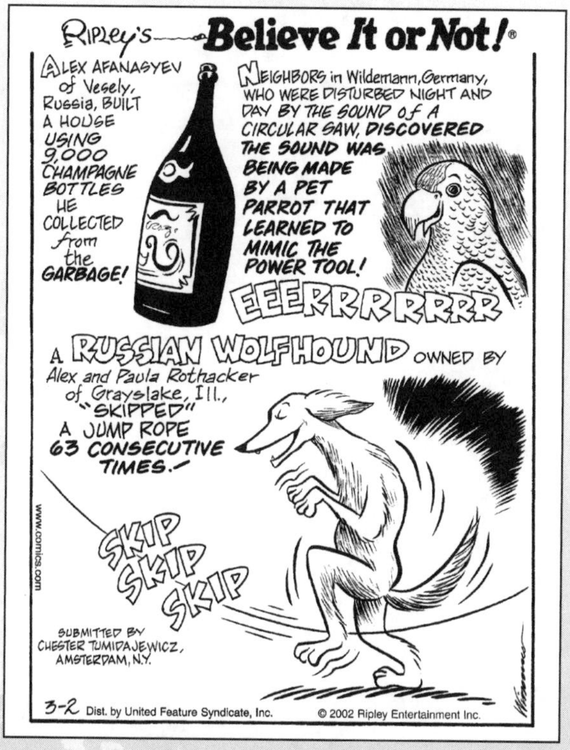
Ripley's Believe It or Not!
ALEX AFANASYEV of Vesely, Russia, BUILT A HOUSE USING 9,000 CHAMPAGNE BOTTLES HE COLLECTED from the GARBAGE!
NEIGHBORS in Wildemann, Germany, WHO WERE DISTURBED NIGHT AND DAY BY THE SOUND of A CIRCULAR SAW, DISCOVERED THE SOUND WAS BEING MADE BY A PET PARROT THAT LEARNED TO MIMIC THE POWER TOOL!
EEERRRRRRR
A RUSSIAN WOLFHOUND OWNED BY Alex and Paula Rothacker of Grayslake, Ill., "SKIPPED" A JUMP ROPE 63 CONSECUTIVE TIMES.
SKIP SKIP SKIP
www.comics.com
SUBMITTED BY CHESTER TUMIDAJEWICZ, AMSTERDAM, N.Y.
3-2 Dist. by United Feature Syndicate, Inc.
© 2002 Ripley Entertainment Inc.

21. In fact, it is has been suggested that Rasputin agreed to visit the Prince after being told that he would be introduced to Yussopov's attractive wife. In many accounts, Rasputin is described as a violent womanizer.

22. Some scholars theorize that Rasputin's hard-drinking lifestyle reduced the acidity of his gastric juices. This acidity actually activates cyanide, the poison that many believe was used in the first attempt to kill Rasputin.

23. Numerous myths surround Houdini's death, but it is now commonly accepted that Houdini did die on October 31st, 1926, of a ruptured appendix. Houdini had evidently been suffering the effects of appendicitis for several days; the actual rupture may have been caused when the escape artist received a blow to the stomach from a college student who was testing Houdini's legendary ability to withstand punches.

24. These were allegedly Houdini's rather cryptic last words.

25. This eulogy is actually composed of pieces from three separate eulogies read at Houdini's funeral. The first quote is from the closing statements by Harry Chesterfield. The second quote was said by Joseph B. Rinn, who was famous for debunking spiritualists and mediums. Houdini has nicknamed Rinn the "Ghost Breaker." The final quote is from Servais Le Roy, who represented the Magician's Club, of which Houdini was president.

26. Dajo did once allow himself to be x-rayed after running a sword through his heart.

27. Some reports claim that Dajo allowed himself to be shot in the head, placed in boiling water, and poisoned, never with any ill effect. Upon his death, an autopsy revealed numerous internal scars showing that Dajo often grazed internal organs during his performances.

28. This was allegedly Houdini's motto.

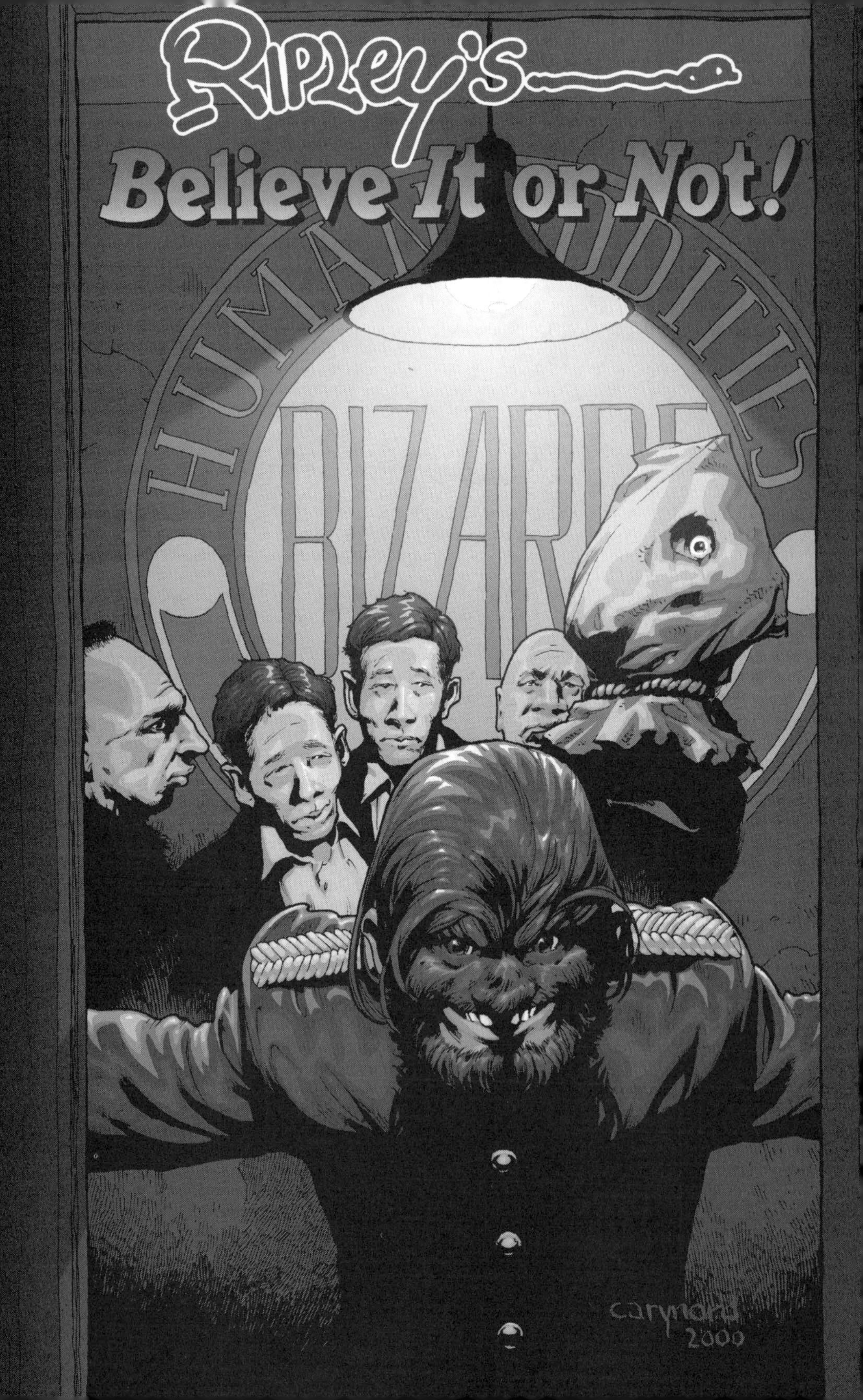
Ripley's
Believe It or Not!

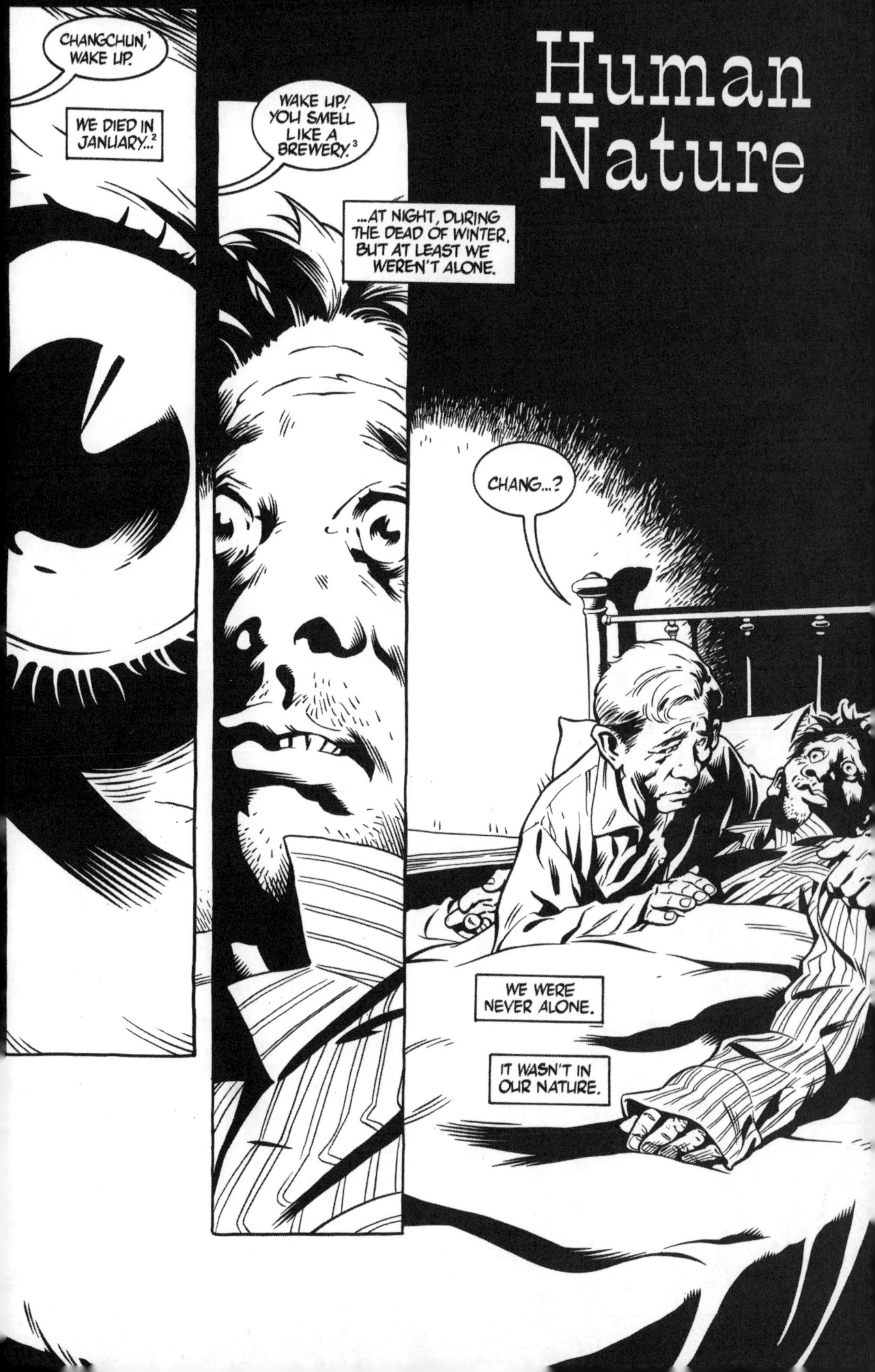
Human Nature
CHANGCHUN,[1] WAKE UP.
WE DIED IN JANUARY...[2]
WAKE UP! YOU SMELL LIKE A BREWERY.[3]
...AT NIGHT, DURING THE DEAD OF WINTER. BUT AT LEAST WE WEREN'T ALONE.
CHANG...?
WE WERE NEVER ALONE.
IT WASN'T IN OUR NATURE.

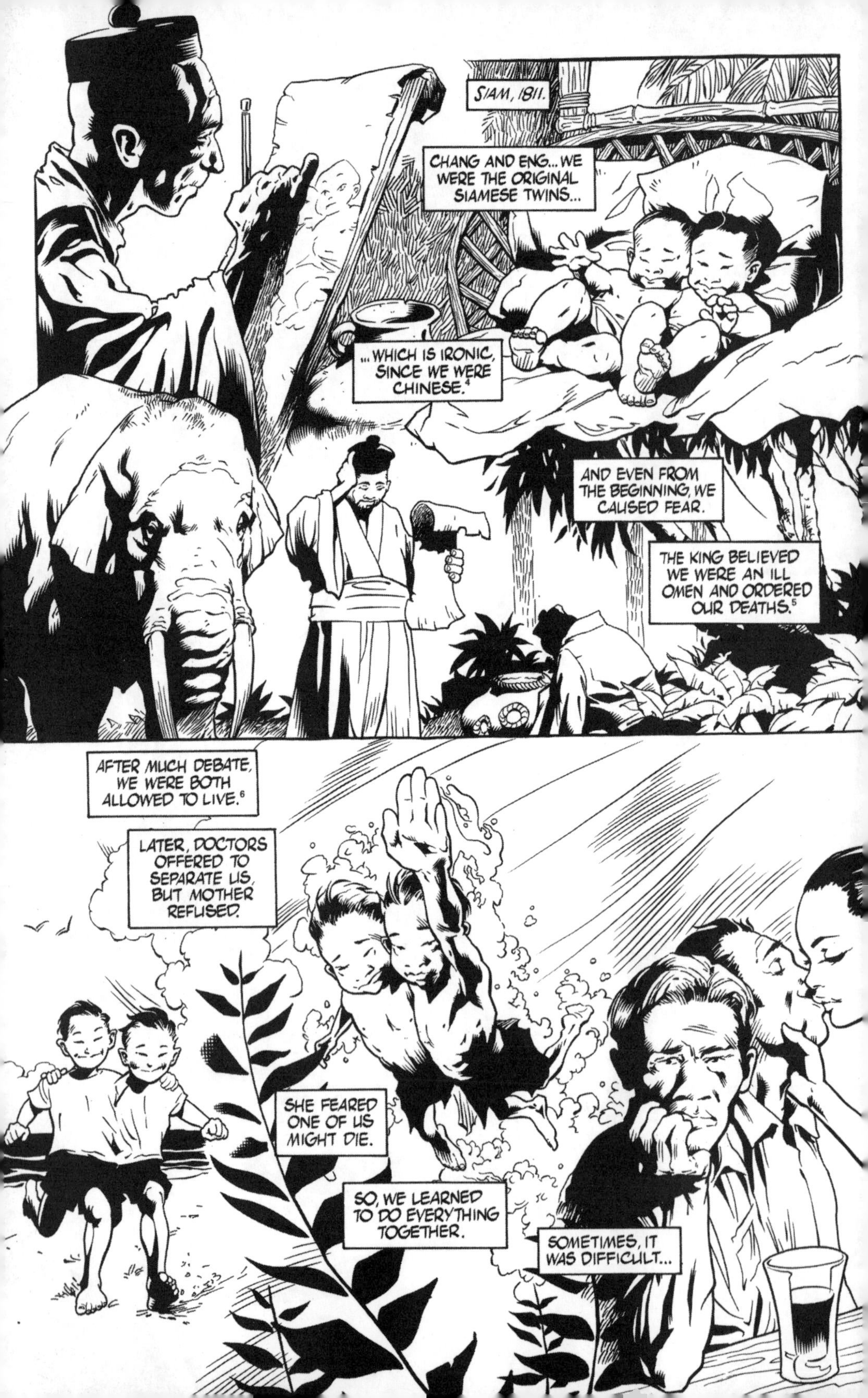
SIAM, 1811.
CHANG AND ENG... WE WERE THE ORIGINAL SIAMESE TWINS...
...WHICH IS IRONIC, SINCE WE WERE CHINESE.[4]
AND EVEN FROM THE BEGINNING, WE CAUSED FEAR.
THE KING BELIEVED WE WERE AN ILL OMEN AND ORDERED OUR DEATHS.[5]
AFTER MUCH DEBATE, WE WERE BOTH ALLOWED TO LIVE.[6]
LATER, DOCTORS OFFERED TO SEPARATE US, BUT MOTHER REFUSED.
SHE FEARED ONE OF US MIGHT DIE.
SO, WE LEARNED TO DO EVERYTHING TOGETHER.
SOMETIMES, IT WAS DIFFICULT...

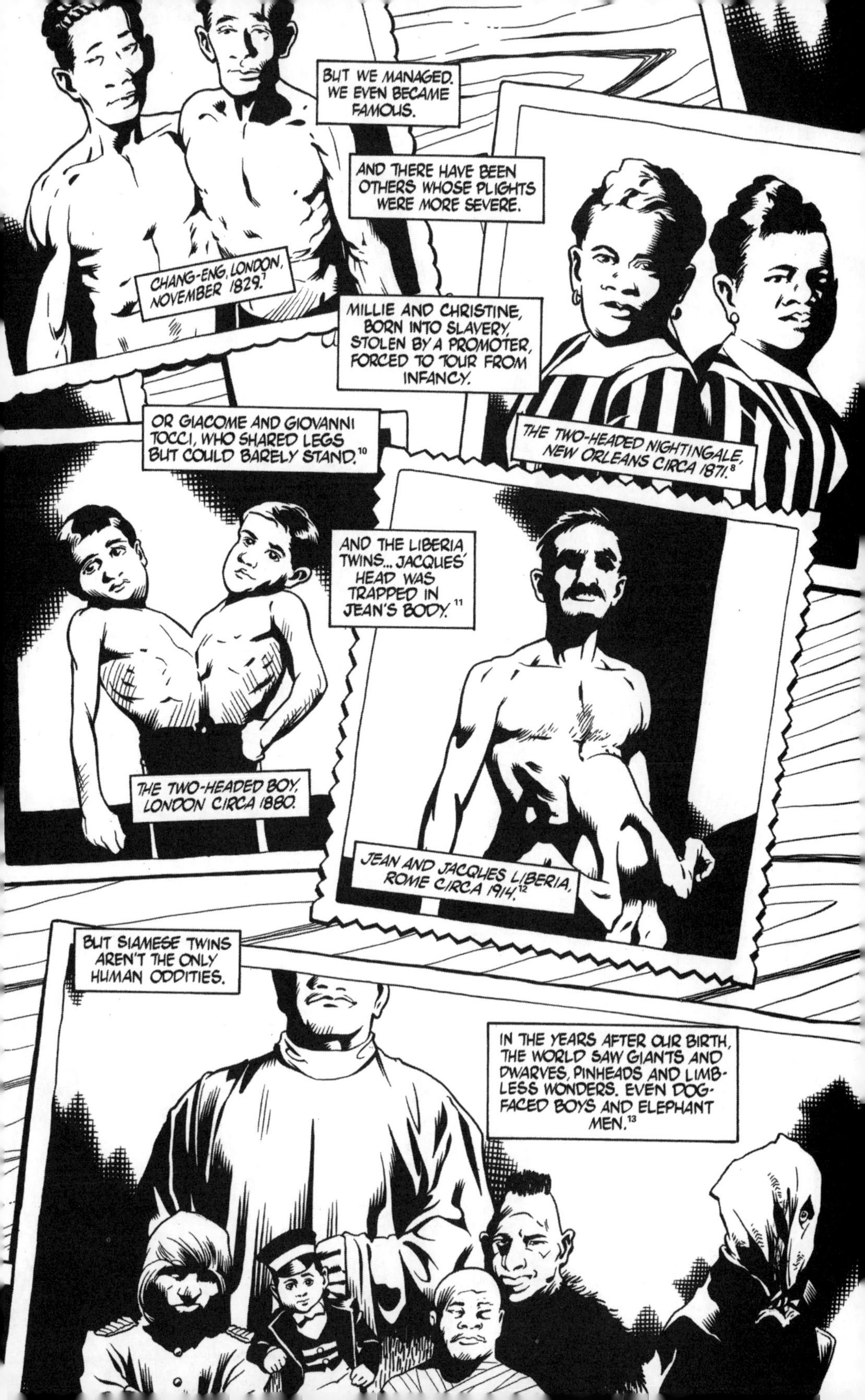
BUT WE MANAGED. WE EVEN BECAME FAMOUS.
AND THERE HAVE BEEN OTHERS WHOSE PLIGHTS WERE MORE SEVERE.
CHANG-ENG, LONDON, NOVEMBER 1829.[7]
MILLIE AND CHRISTINE, BORN INTO SLAVERY, STOLEN BY A PROMOTER, FORCED TO TOUR FROM INFANCY.
THE TWO-HEADED NIGHTINGALE, NEW ORLEANS CIRCA 1871.[8]
OR GIACOME AND GIOVANNI TOCCI, WHO SHARED LEGS BUT COULD BARELY STAND.[10]
AND THE LIBERIA TWINS... JACQUES' HEAD WAS TRAPPED IN JEAN'S BODY.[11]
THE TWO-HEADED BOY, LONDON CIRCA 1880.
JEAN AND JACQUES LIBERIA, ROME CIRCA 1914.[12]
BUT SIAMESE TWINS AREN'T THE ONLY HUMAN ODDITIES.
IN THE YEARS AFTER OUR BIRTH, THE WORLD SAW GIANTS AND DWARVES, PINHEADS AND LIMB-LESS WONDERS. EVEN DOG-FACED BOYS AND ELEPHANT MEN.[13]

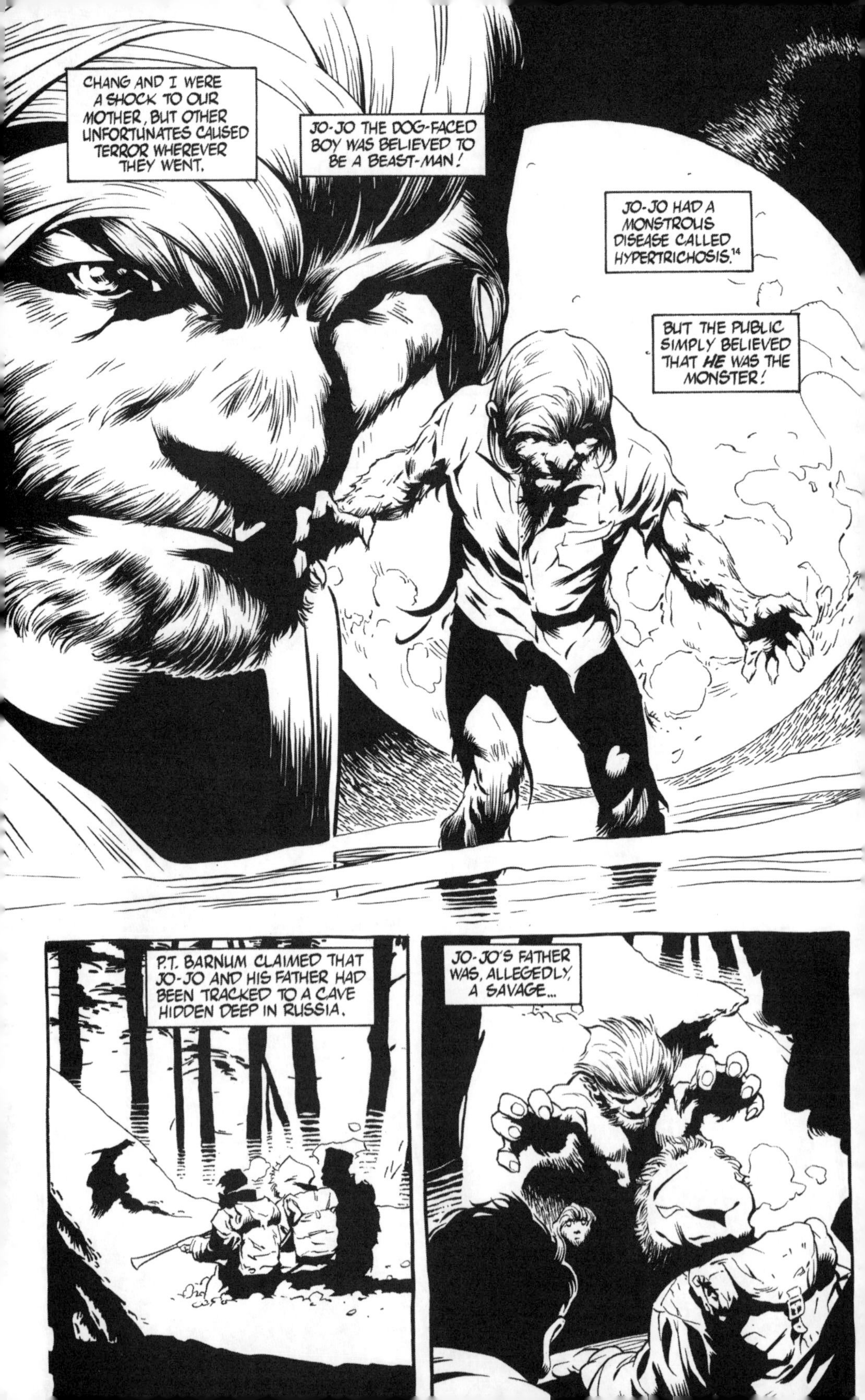
CHANG AND I WERE A SHOCK TO OUR MOTHER, BUT OTHER UNFORTUNATES CAUSED TERROR WHEREVER THEY WENT.
JO-JO THE DOG-FACED BOY WAS BELIEVED TO BE A BEAST-MAN!
JO-JO HAD A MONSTROUS DISEASE CALLED HYPERTRICHOSIS.[14]
BUT THE PUBLIC SIMPLY BELIEVED THAT *HE* WAS THE MONSTER!
P.T. BARNUM CLAIMED THAT JO-JO AND HIS FATHER HAD BEEN TRACKED TO A CAVE HIDDEN DEEP IN RUSSIA.
JO-JO'S FATHER WAS, ALLEGEDLY, A SAVAGE...

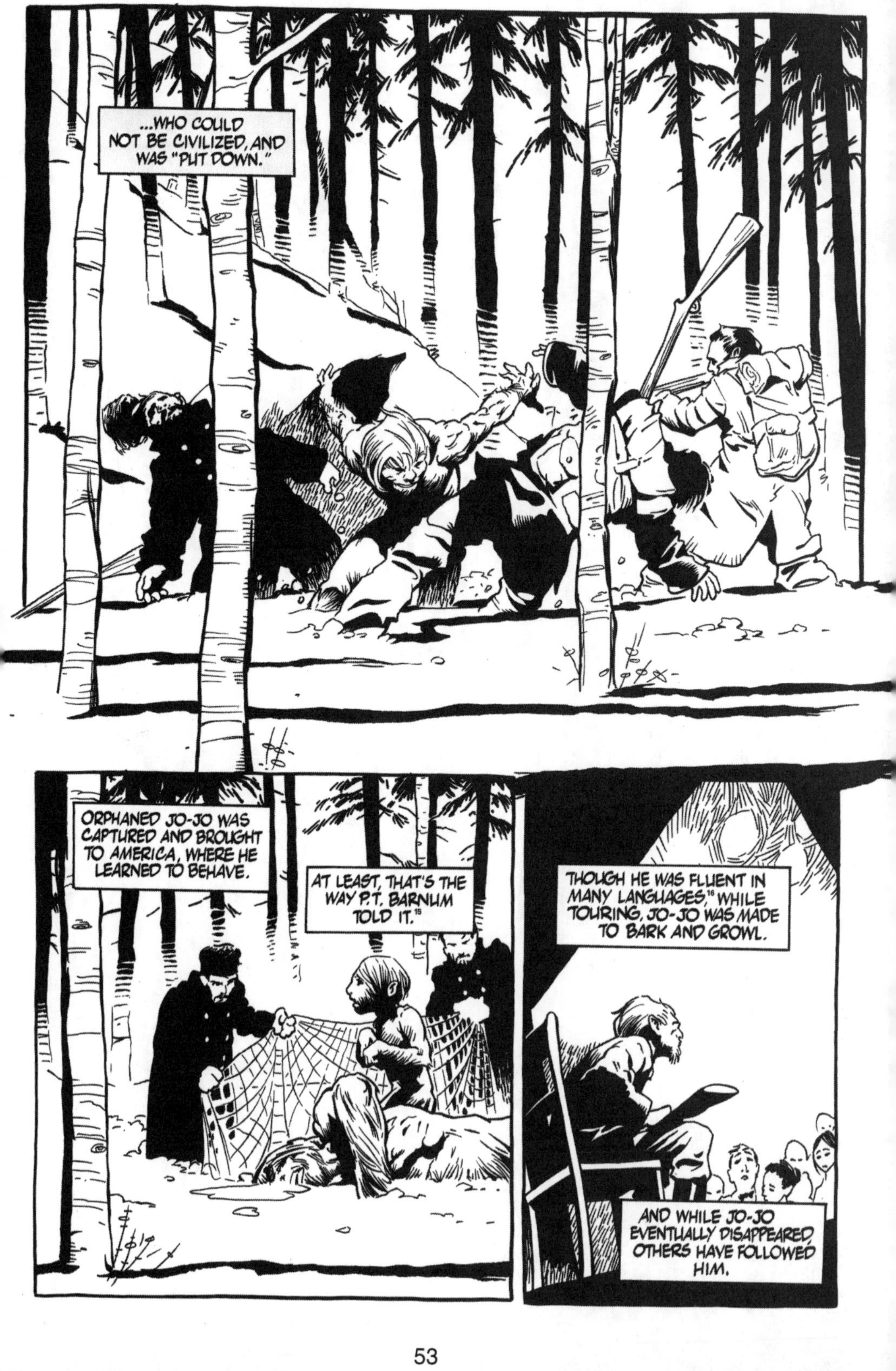
...WHO COULD NOT BE CIVILIZED, AND WAS "PUT DOWN."
ORPHANED JO-JO WAS CAPTURED AND BROUGHT TO AMERICA, WHERE HE LEARNED TO BEHAVE.
AT LEAST, THAT'S THE WAY P.T. BARNUM TOLD IT.[15]
THOUGH HE WAS FLUENT IN MANY LANGUAGES,[16] WHILE TOURING, JO-JO WAS MADE TO BARK AND GROWL.
AND WHILE JO-JO EVENTUALLY DISAPPEARED, OTHERS HAVE FOLLOWED HIM.

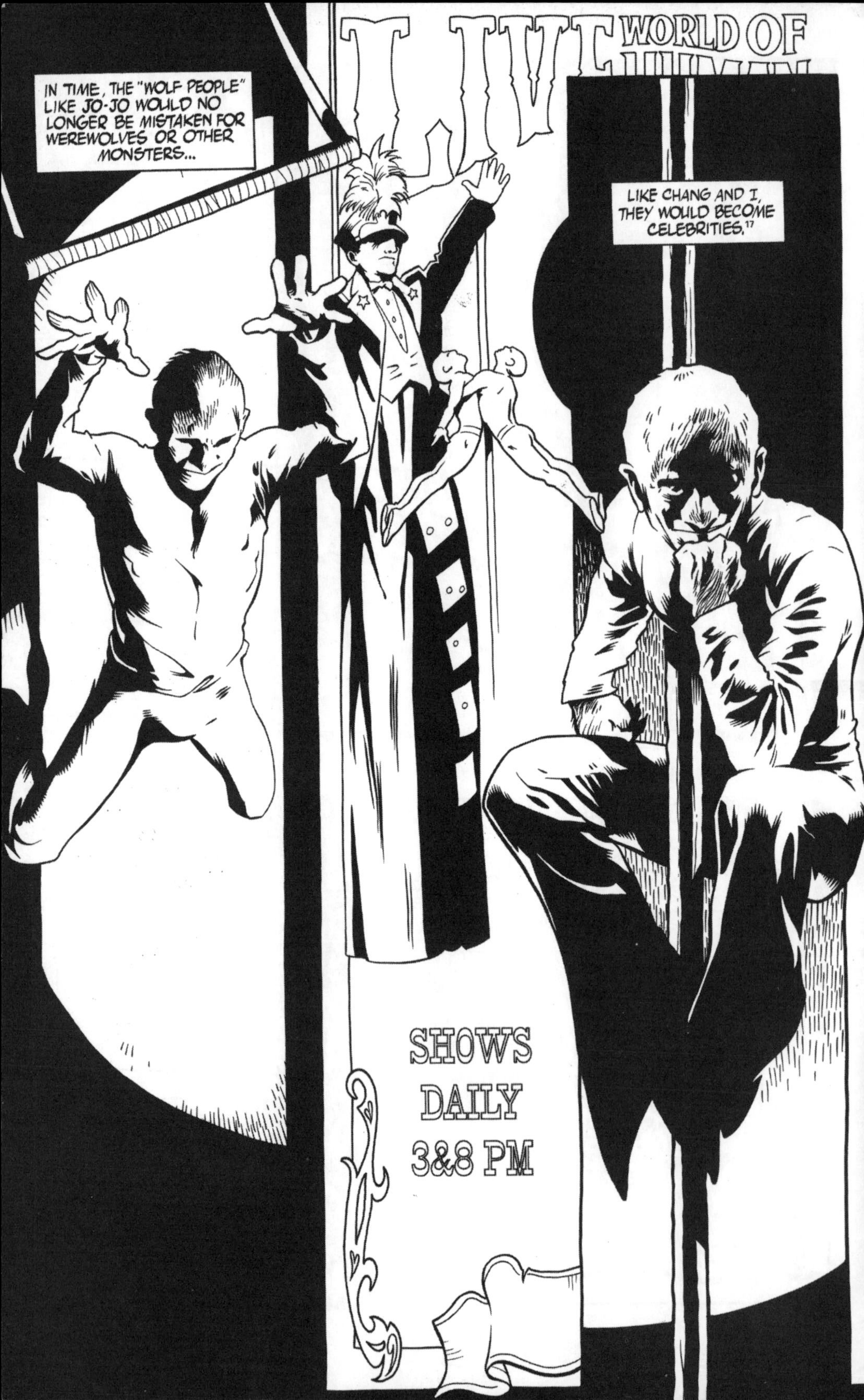
IN TIME, THE "WOLF PEOPLE" LIKE JO-JO WOULD NO LONGER BE MISTAKEN FOR WEREWOLVES OR OTHER MONSTERS...
WORLD OF
LIKE CHANG AND I, THEY WOULD BECOME CELEBRITIES.[17]
SHOWS DAILY 3&8 PM

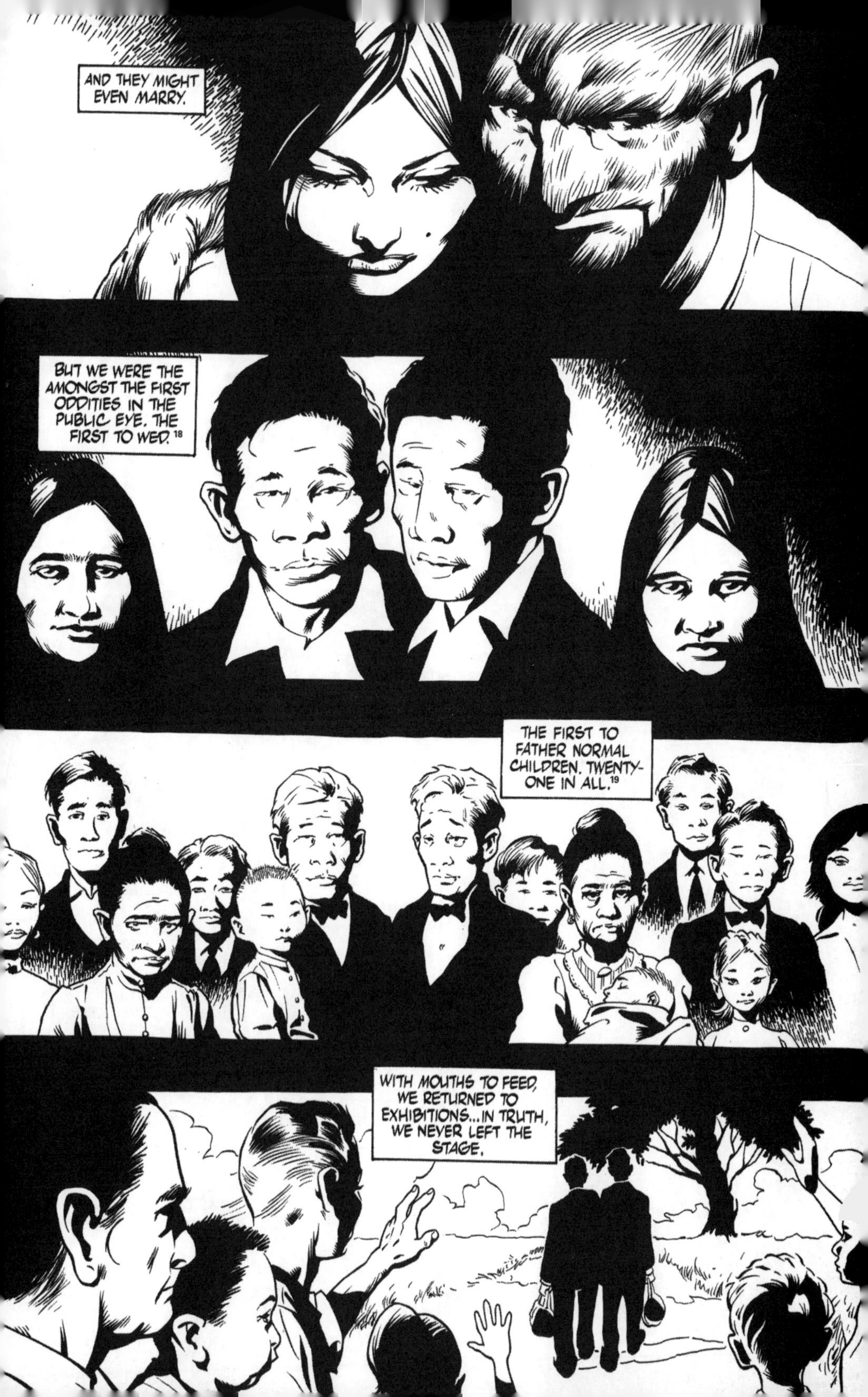
AND THEY MIGHT EVEN MARRY.
BUT WE WERE THE AMONGST THE FIRST ODDITIES IN THE PUBLIC EYE. THE FIRST TO WED.[18]
THE FIRST TO FATHER NORMAL CHILDREN. TWENTY-ONE IN ALL.[19]
WITH MOUTHS TO FEED, WE RETURNED TO EXHIBITIONS...IN TRUTH, WE NEVER LEFT THE STAGE.

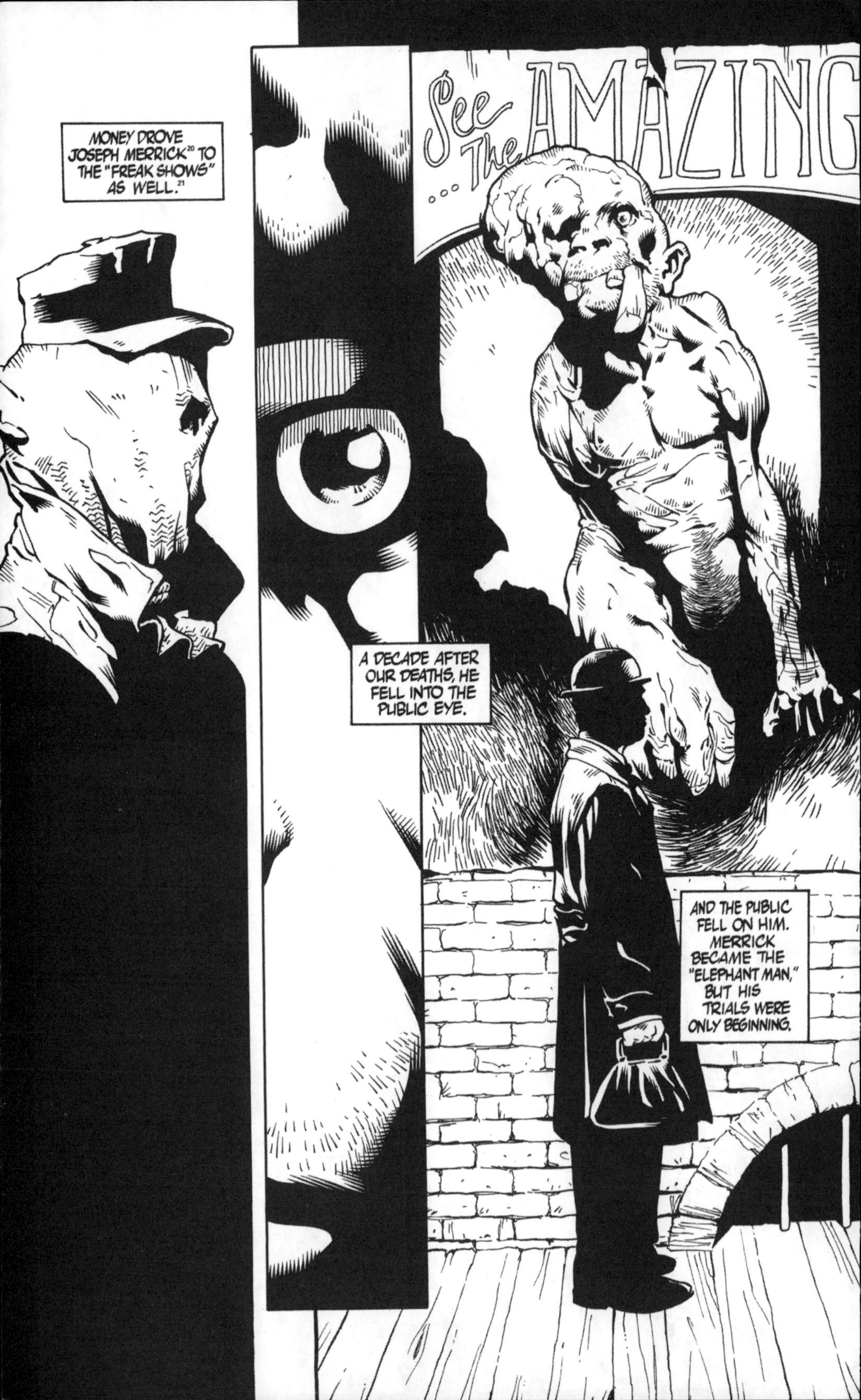
MONEY DROVE JOSEPH MERRICK[20] TO THE "FREAK SHOWS" AS WELL.[21]
See The AMAZING
...
A DECADE AFTER OUR DEATHS, HE FELL INTO THE PUBLIC EYE.
AND THE PUBLIC FELL ON HIM. MERRICK BECAME THE "ELEPHANT MAN," BUT HIS TRIALS WERE ONLY BEGINNING.

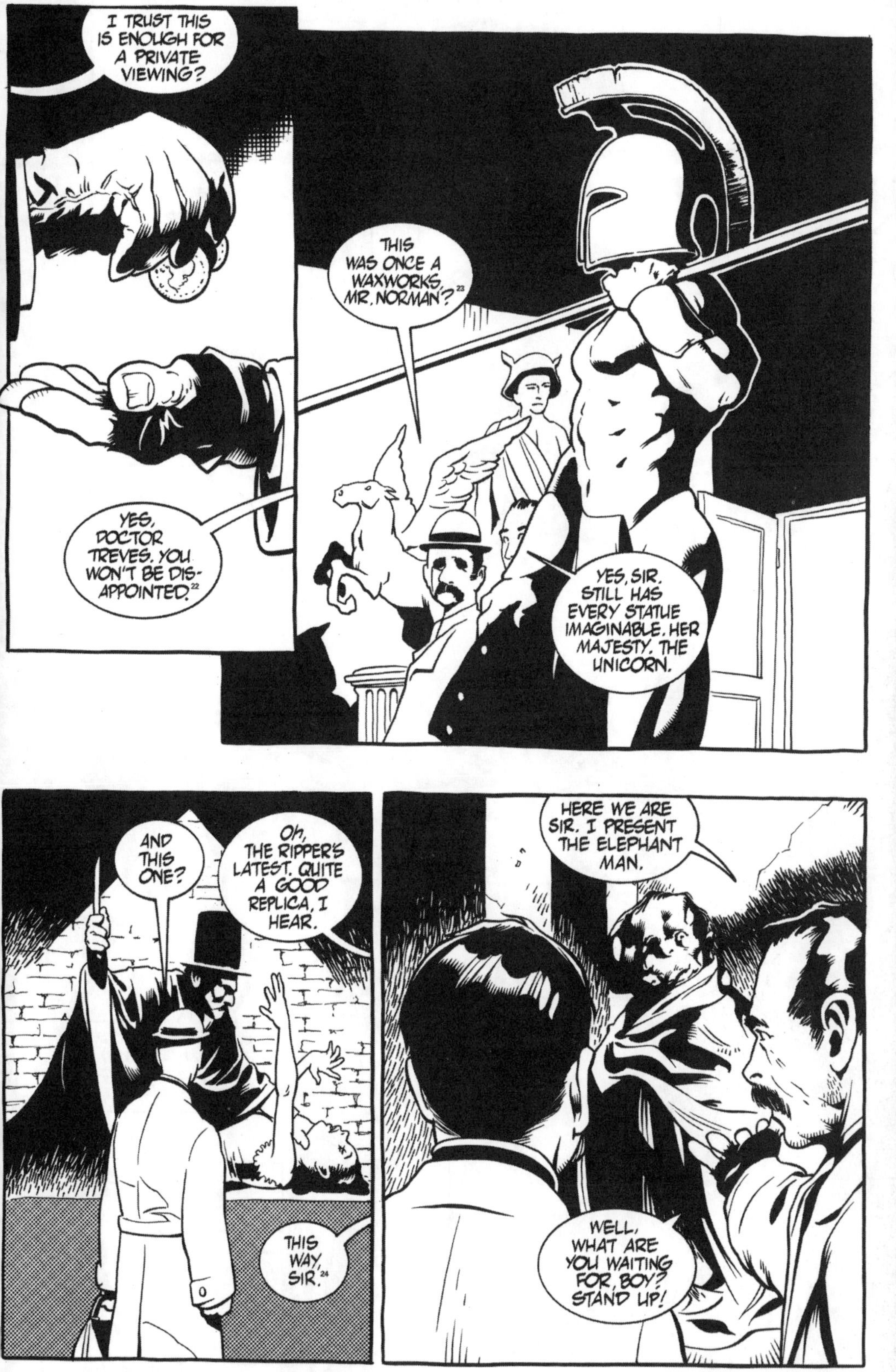
I TRUST THIS IS ENOUGH FOR A PRIVATE VIEWING?
YES, DOCTOR TREVES. YOU WON'T BE DIS-APPOINTED.[22]
THIS WAS ONCE A WAXWORKS, MR. NORMAN?[23]
YES, SIR. STILL HAS EVERY STATUE IMAGINABLE. HER MAJESTY. THE UNICORN.
AND THIS ONE?
Oh, THE RIPPER'S LATEST. QUITE A GOOD REPLICA, I HEAR.
THIS WAY, SIR.[24]
HERE WE ARE SIR. I PRESENT THE ELEPHANT MAN.
WELL, WHAT ARE YOU WAITING FOR, BOY? STAND UP!

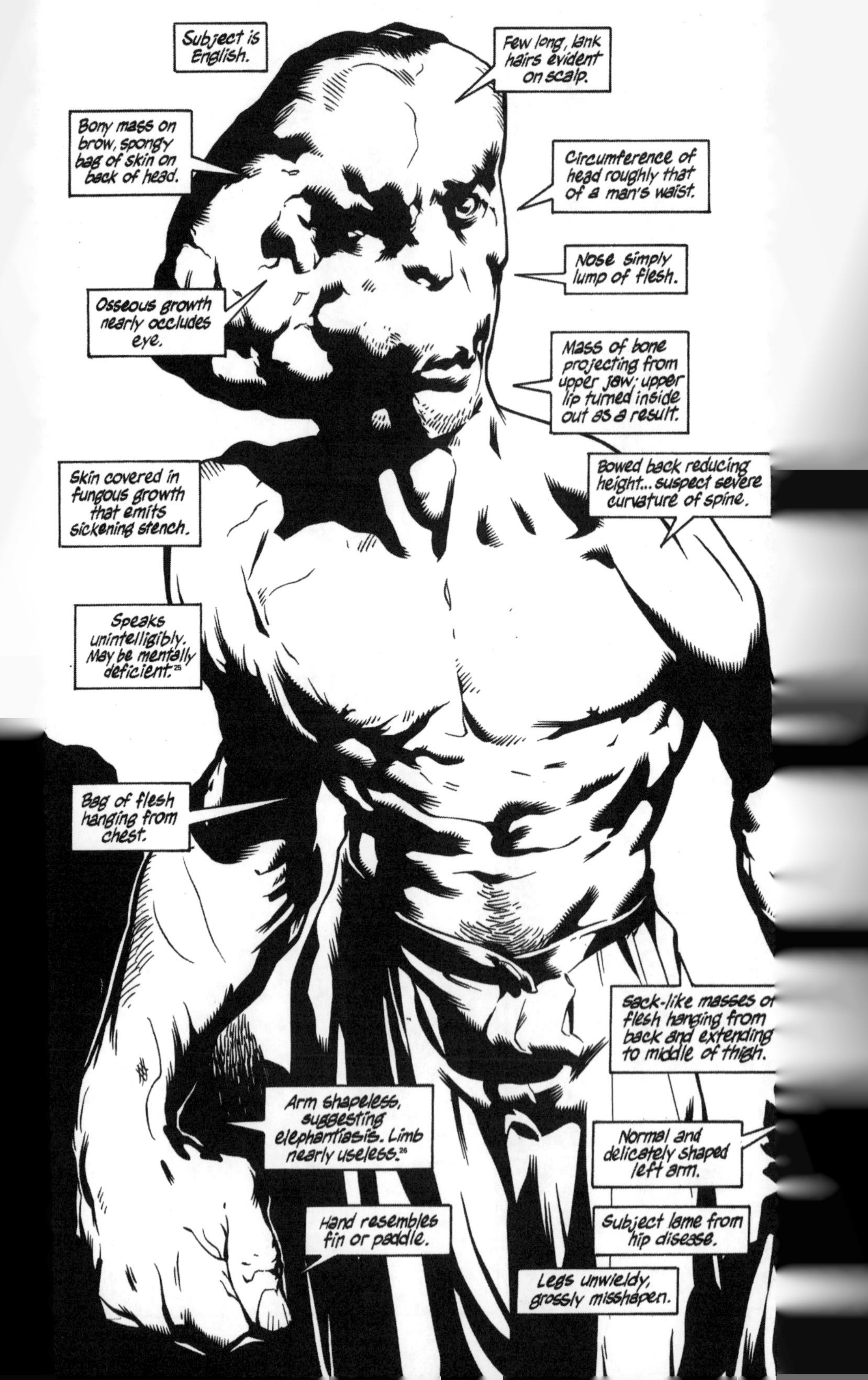

Subject is English.
Few long, lank hairs evident on scalp.
Bony mass on brow, spongy bag of skin on back of head.
Circumference of head roughly that of a man's waist.
Nose simply lump of flesh.
Osseous growth nearly occludes eye.
Mass of bone projecting from upper jaw; upper lip turned inside out as a result.
Skin covered in fungous growth that emits sickening stench.
Bowed back reducing height... suspect severe curvature of spine.
Speaks unintelligibly. May be mentally deficient.[25]
Bag of flesh hanging from chest.
Sack-like masses of flesh hanging from back and extending to middle of thigh.
Arm shapeless, suggesting elephantiasis. Limb nearly useless.[26]
Normal and delicately shaped left arm.
Hand resembles fin or paddle.
Subject lame from hip disease.
Legs unwieldy, grossly misshapen.

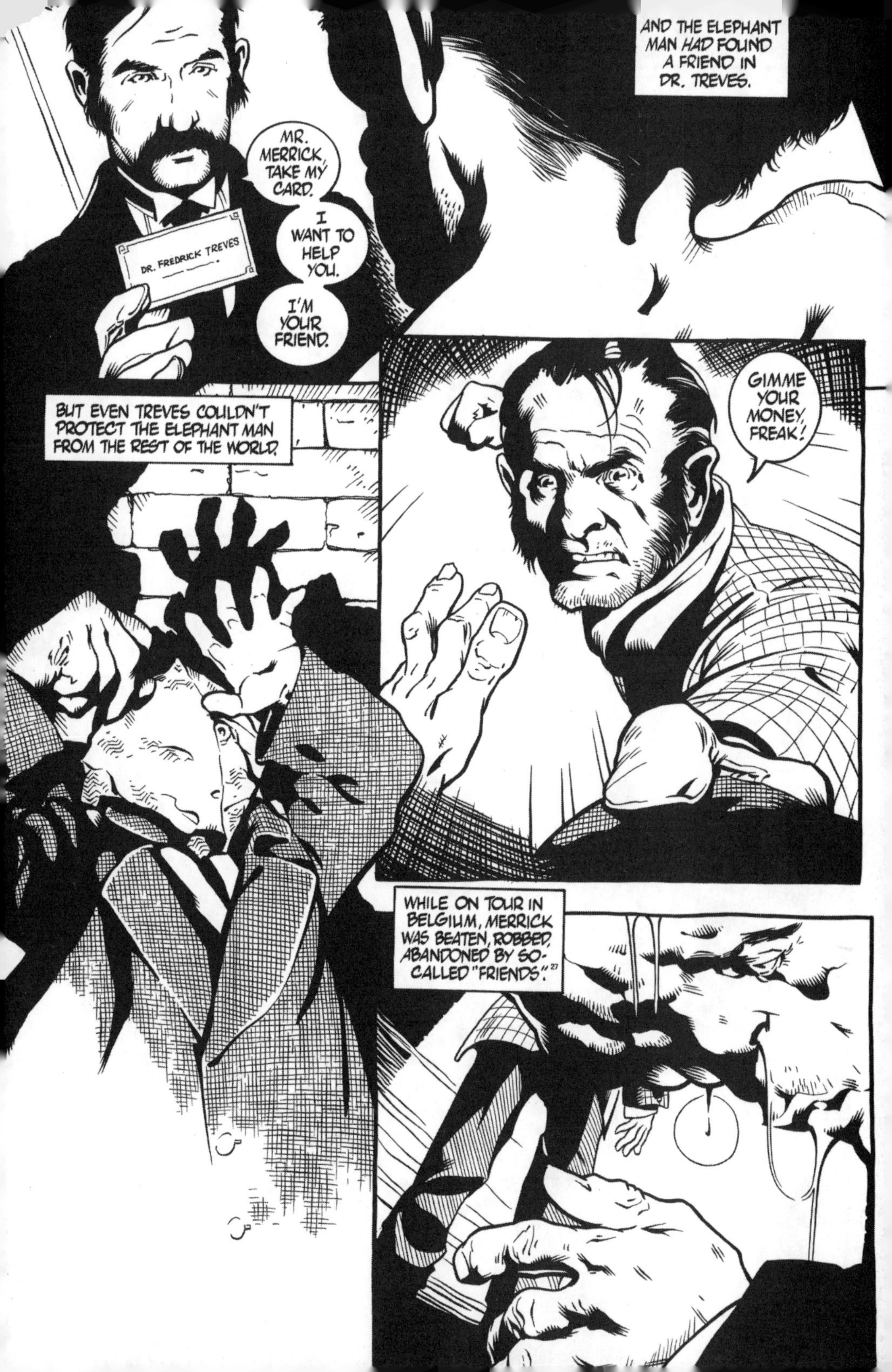
AND THE ELEPHANT MAN *HAD* FOUND A FRIEND IN DR. TREVES.
MR. MERRICK, TAKE MY CARD.
I WANT TO HELP YOU.
I'M YOUR FRIEND.
DR. FREDRICK TREVES
BUT EVEN TREVES COULDN'T PROTECT THE ELEPHANT MAN FROM THE REST OF THE WORLD.
GIMME YOUR MONEY, FREAK!
WHILE ON TOUR IN BELGIUM, MERRICK WAS BEATEN, ROBBED, ABANDONED BY SO-CALLED "FRIENDS."[27]

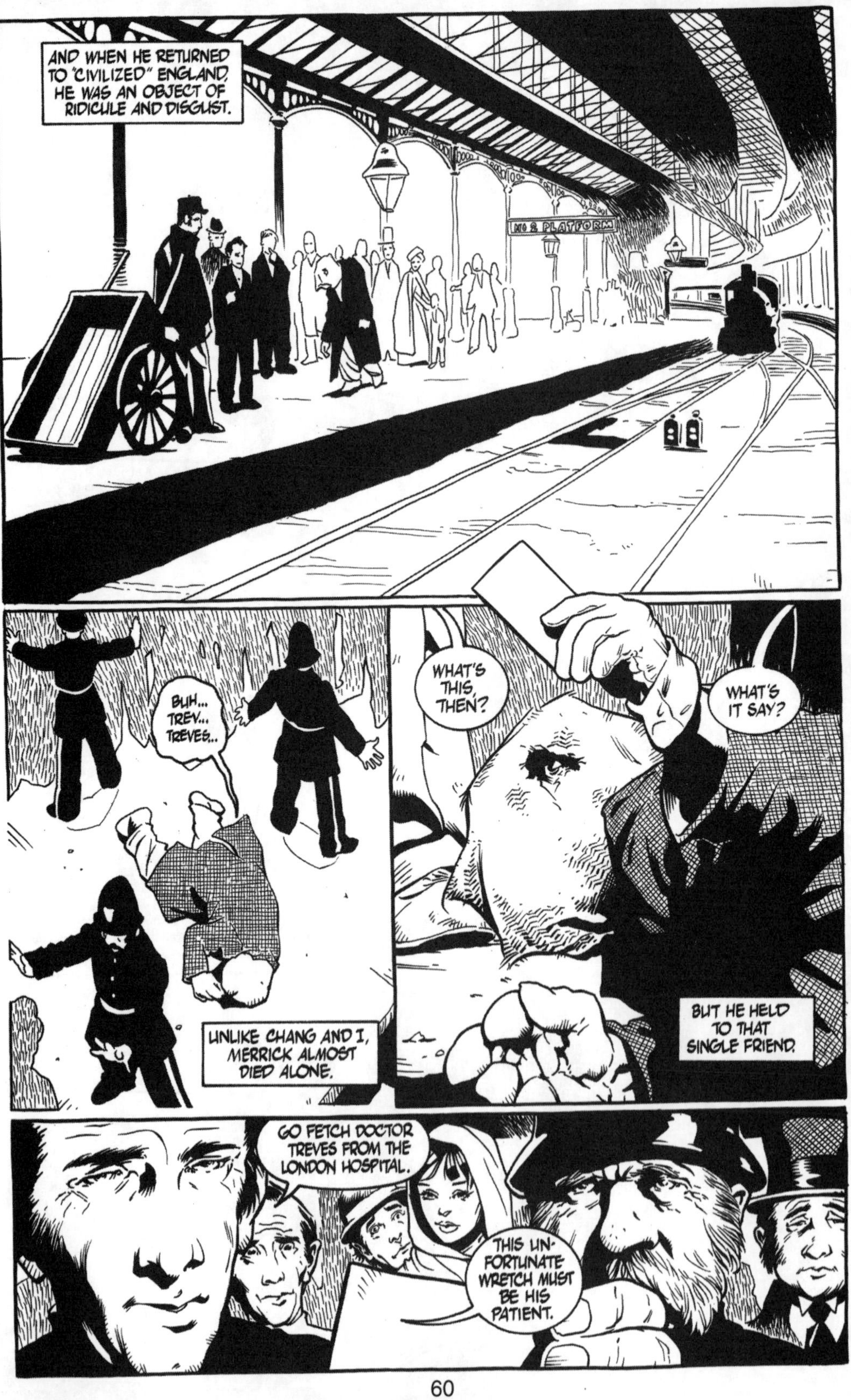
AND WHEN HE RETURNED TO "CIVILIZED" ENGLAND, HE WAS AN OBJECT OF RIDICULE AND DISGUST.
No 2 PLATFORM
BUH... TREV... TREVES...
UNLIKE CHANG AND I, MERRICK ALMOST DIED ALONE.
WHAT'S THIS, THEN?
WHAT'S IT SAY?
BUT HE HELD TO THAT SINGLE FRIEND.
GO FETCH DOCTOR TREVES FROM THE LONDON HOSPITAL.
THIS UNFORTUNATE WRETCH MUST BE HIS PATIENT.

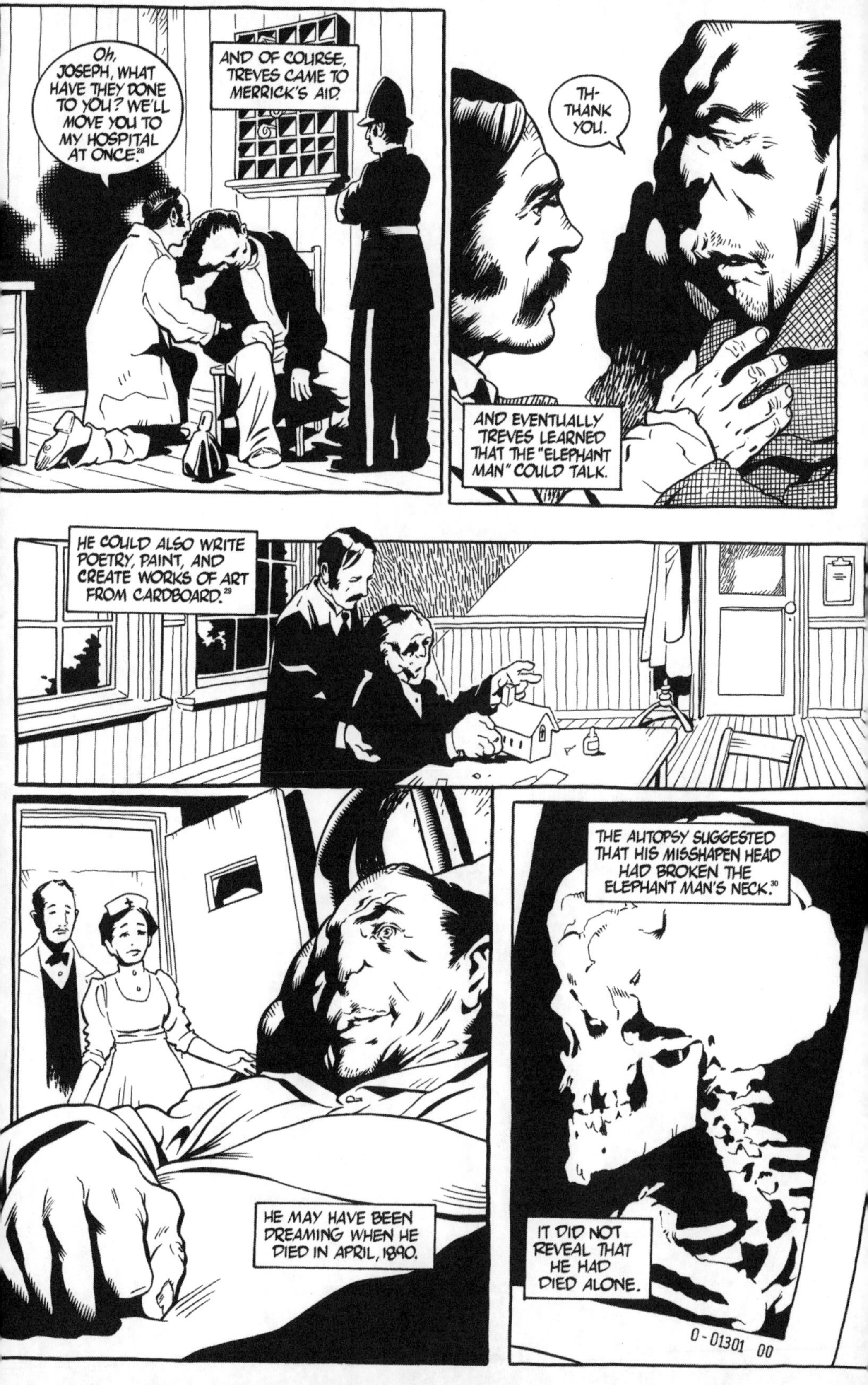

Oh, JOSEPH, WHAT HAVE THEY DONE TO YOU? WE'LL MOVE YOU TO MY HOSPITAL AT ONCE.[28]
AND OF COURSE, TREVES CAME TO MERRICK'S AID.
TH-THANK YOU.
AND EVENTUALLY TREVES LEARNED THAT THE "ELEPHANT MAN" COULD TALK.
HE COULD ALSO WRITE POETRY, PAINT, AND CREATE WORKS OF ART FROM CARDBOARD.[29]
HE MAY HAVE BEEN DREAMING WHEN HE DIED IN APRIL, 1890.
THE AUTOPSY SUGGESTED THAT HIS MISSHAPEN HEAD HAD BROKEN THE ELEPHANT MAN'S NECK.[30]
IT DID NOT REVEAL THAT HE HAD DIED ALONE.

0-01301 00

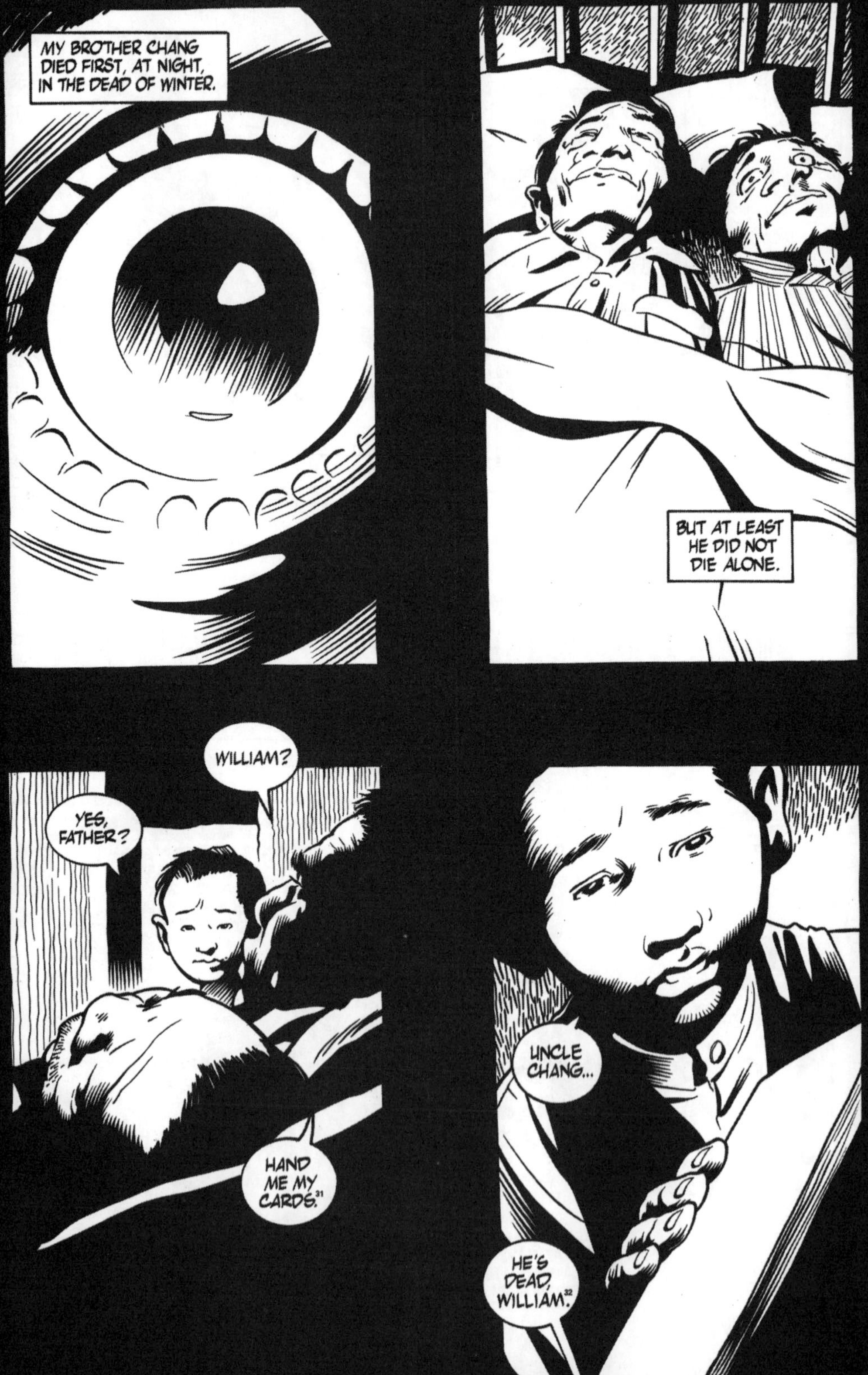

MY BROTHER CHANG DIED FIRST, AT NIGHT, IN THE DEAD OF WINTER.
BUT AT LEAST HE DID NOT DIE ALONE.
WILLIAM?
YES, FATHER?
HAND ME MY CARDS.[31]
UNCLE CHANG...
HE'S DEAD, WILLIAM.[32]

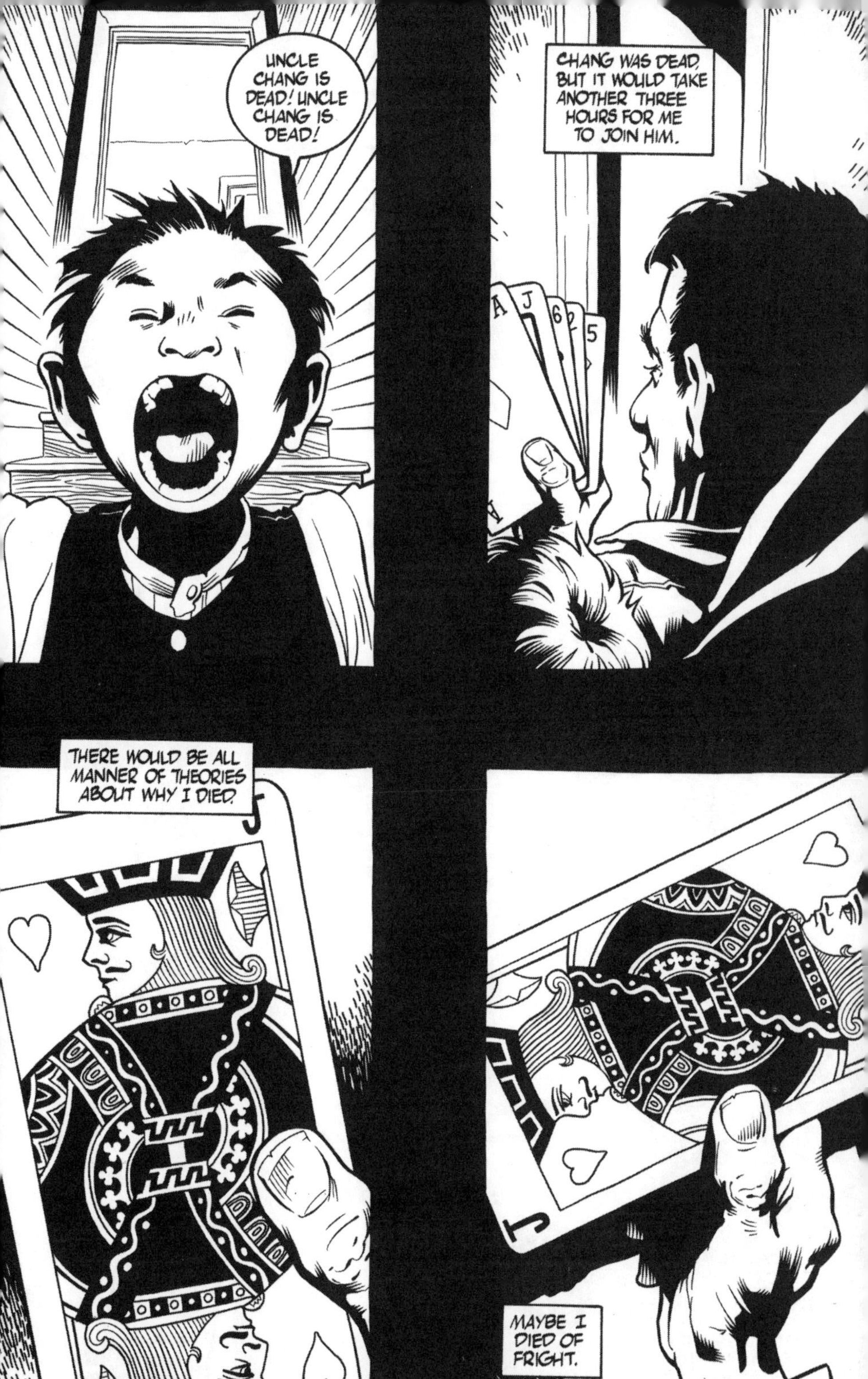
UNCLE CHANG IS DEAD! UNCLE CHANG IS DEAD!
CHANG WAS DEAD, BUT IT WOULD TAKE ANOTHER THREE HOURS FOR ME TO JOIN HIM.
THERE WOULD BE ALL MANNER OF THEORIES ABOUT WHY I DIED.
MAYBE I DIED OF FRIGHT.

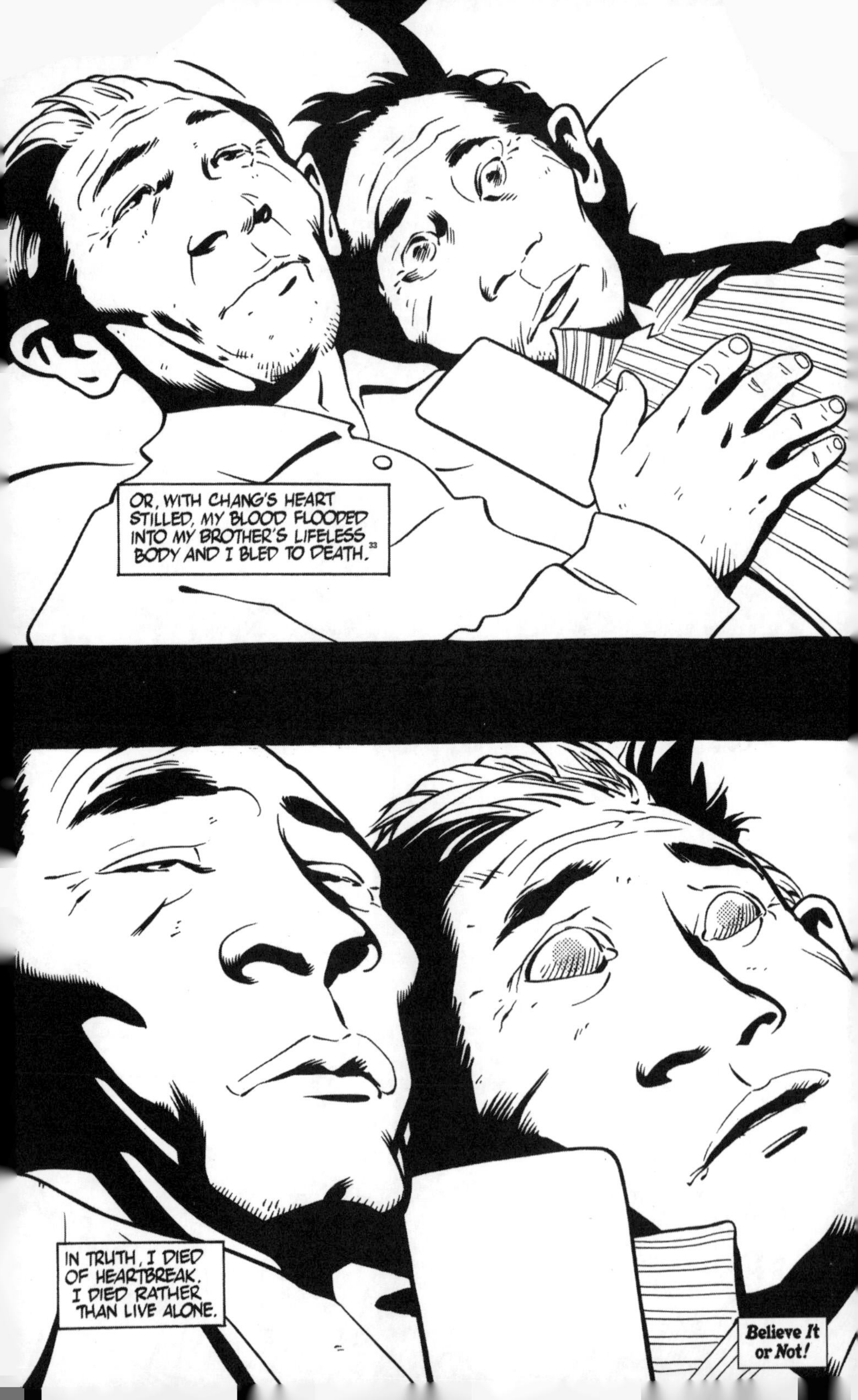
OR, WITH CHANG'S HEART STILLED, MY BLOOD FLOODED INTO MY BROTHER'S LIFELESS BODY AND I BLED TO DEATH.[33]
IN TRUTH, I DIED OF HEARTBREAK. I DIED RATHER THAN LIVE ALONE.
Believe It or Not!

HUMAN NATURE NOTES

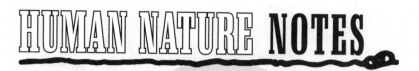

1. Chang's given name was "ChangChun," while Eng's was "Eng-in." They shortened their names to simply "Chang" and "Eng."

2. The twins died late at night on January 16 or in the early morning of January 17, 1874.

3. Prior to his death, Chang had become a heavy whiskey drinker, which is often cited as a contributing factor to his generally poor health and ultimate demise.

4. Chang and Eng were born in Siam in 1811 to a Chinese father and half Chinese, half Malaysian mother.

5. The King of Siam in 1811 was Rama II (Phra Buddha Lertla Napalai, the 2nd King of the Chakri Dynasty), who had risen to the throne only two years prior to Eng and Chang's birth.

6. Although King Rama II initially ordered the deaths of the twins, it's unclear why this order was never carried out. King Rama II was a devout Buddhist, and some researchers claim this faith caused him to rethink his decree. Others hold that Rama II was only waiting for some kind of disaster to strike; when none occurred, the King understood that the twins were not an evil sign and allowed them to live.

7. In 1829, a British merchant named Robert Hunter and his partner Captain Able Coffin convinced the twins' mother and the King of Siam to allow Chang and Eng to tour the world. The boys were "managed" by Hunter and Coffin on a tour of the eastern United States and London. In many ads, they were billed as "Chang-Eng" as if one entity.

Ripley's Believe It or Not!®
ROS Llewellyn BOUGHT A WOODEN BEACH HUT in Dorset, England, for $180,000! Believe It or Not!
THE PREVIOUS OWNERS PAID $135 for THE 68-YR.-OLD HUT!
... A FRESH COAT OF PAINT WOULD DO WONDERS!
HENRY MEREDITH of London, Ont., Canada, HAS A COLLECTION of OVER 2,800 MUSICAL INSTRUMENTS IN HIS HOME, INCLUDING A TIBETAN TRUMPET MADE from A HUMAN THIGH BONE!
www.comics.com
© 2002 Ripley Entertainment Inc.
Dist. by United Feature Syndicate, Inc.
2-27

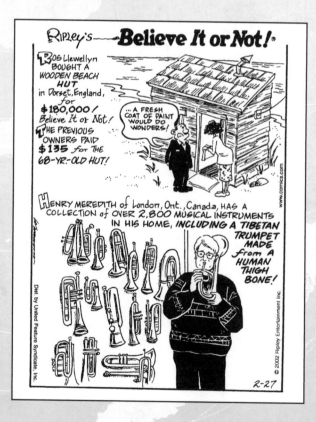

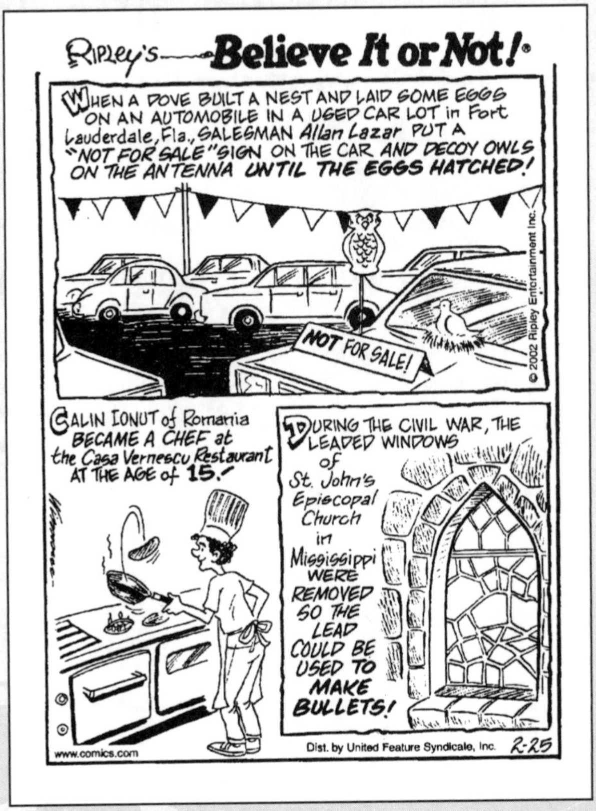
RIPLEY'S Believe It or Not!
WHEN A DOVE BUILT A NEST AND LAID SOME EGGS ON AN AUTOMOBILE IN A USED CAR LOT in Fort Lauderdale, Fla., SALESMAN Allan Lazar PUT A "NOT FOR SALE" SIGN ON THE CAR AND DECOY OWLS ON THE ANTENNA UNTIL THE EGGS HATCHED!
NOT FOR SALE!
© 2002 Ripley Entertainment Inc.
CALIN IONUT of Romania BECAME A CHEF at the Casa Vernescu Restaurant AT THE AGE of 15!
DURING THE CIVIL WAR, THE LEADED WINDOWS of St. John's Episcopal Church in Mississippi WERE REMOVED SO THE LEAD COULD BE USED TO MAKE BULLETS!
www.comics.com
Dist. by United Feature Syndicate, Inc.
2-25

8. Millie and Christine McCoy were also labeled the "Two-Headed Girl." They continued in show business after the Civil War, but retired around 1900. While Chang and Eng may have been aware of Millie and Christine, other characters in this story came to prominence or were born after Chang and Eng's death. Obviously, Eng has been watching the world from beyond the grave...

9. The Tocci twins were joined at the sixth rib and shared lower extremities. By all accounts, they were too weak to stand without aid. It's widely believe that they were the inspiration for Mark Twain's *Pudd'Nhead Wilson*.

10. The Tocci twins were born in 1875 and exhibited throughout the United States and Europe from the time they were about one month old. They retired in their late teens and lived out the rest of their lives in seclusion (although they did marry). While touring, they were also known as the "Blended Twins."

11. Jean Libbera was born with a miniature twin growing from his abdomen. He named it Jacques, although the twin exhibited no signs of life on its own. A German doctor who X-rayed Jean claimed that Jacques did have a malformed head embedded in Jean's body.

12. Jean Libbera was one of the highest paid performers of his time.

13. Pictured in this panel are (right from left): Jo-Jo, the Dog-faced Boy; Chang, the Chinese Giant; General Tom Thumb; Zip the Pinhead; Prince Randian, the Limbless Man; and Joseph Merrick. With the exception of Chang the Giant and Merrick, all of the other personalities were "discovered" by P.T. Barnum. Incidentially, the Siamese Twins also toured with Barnum at one point.

14. Hypertrichosis is a disease that causes the growth of excessive hair all over the body, including the face. It afflicts both men and women.

15. In actuality, it's believed that Jo-Jo was born in St. Petersburg and may have toured with his father there, before his father's death.

16. By most accounts, Jo-Jo could speak Russian, German, and English.

17. The two acrobatic images on this page were inspired by the feats of the real life "wolf brothers" Larry (Gabriel Ramos Gomez) and Danny (Victor Ramon Ramos Gomez), who have performed at Ripley's Believe-it-or-Not! events.

18. Chang and Eng married Adelaide (Addie) and Sarah (or Sally) Yates (respectively) in 1843. Chang and Eng were both 44; the sisters were in their late 20s.

19. Eng fathered 11 children, while Chang fathered 10. None of the children were twins.

20. Merrick's given name was "Joseph Carey Merrick," likely after his father, who was also named Joseph. Curiously, his first name is sometimes given as "John," which is the name used in the 1980 film about the so-called "elephant man." This error can probably be attributed to the fact that Dr. Frederick Treves, who wrote extensively about the Elephant Man, misunderstood Joseph's name on their first meeting and called him simply "John."

21. Merrick was destitute when, in 1884, he agreed to begin sideshow appearances. He was in his very early 20s.

22. Dr. Frederick Treves met Joseph in 1884, shortly after Merrick began performing in a London sideshow. He studied Merrick extensively until the Elephant Man's death.

23. Tom Norman was Joseph Merrick's first promoter, arranging "showings" of the Elephant Man in the Whitechapel area of London. Although he has been vilified in other sources, there's no indication that Norman ever physically abused Merrick.

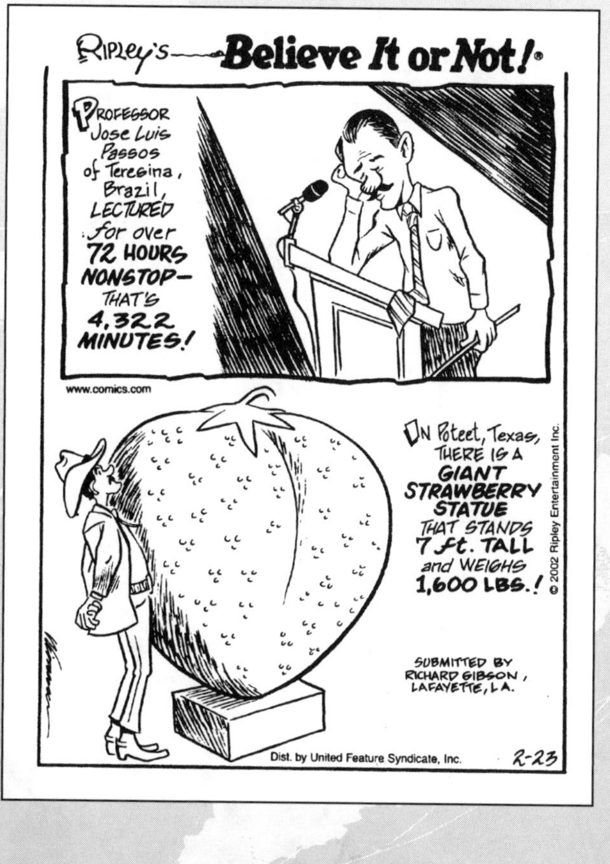

Ripley's Believe It or Not!
Professor Jose Luis Passos of Teresina, Brazil, LECTURED for over 72 HOURS NONSTOP— THAT'S 4,322 MINUTES!
www.comics.com
In Poteet, Texas, THERE IS A GIANT STRAWBERRY STATUE THAT STANDS 7 ft. TALL and WEIGHS 1,600 LBS.!
© 2002 Ripley Entertainment Inc.
SUBMITTED BY RICHARD GIBSON, LAFAYETTE, LA.
Dist. by United Feature Syndicate, Inc.
2-23

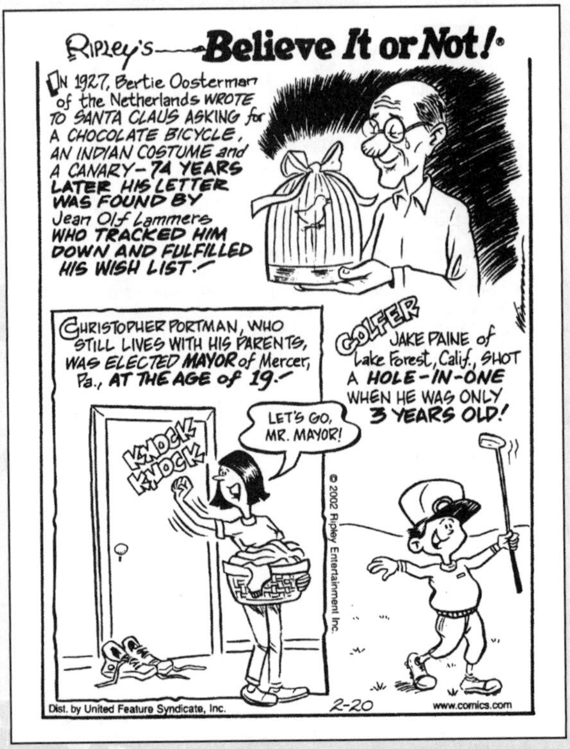
Ripley's Believe It or Not!
IN 1927, Bertie Oosterman of the Netherlands WROTE TO SANTA CLAUS ASKING for A CHOCOLATE BICYCLE, AN INDIAN COSTUME and A CANARY—74 YEARS LATER HIS LETTER WAS FOUND BY Jean Olf Lammers WHO TRACKED HIM DOWN AND FULFILLED HIS WISH LIST.
CHRISTOPHER PORTMAN, WHO STILL LIVES WITH HIS PARENTS, WAS ELECTED MAYOR of Mercer, Pa., AT THE AGE of 19.
KNOCK KNOCK
LET'S GO, MR. MAYOR!
GOLFER JAKE PAINE of Lake Forest, Calif., SHOT A HOLE-IN-ONE WHEN HE WAS ONLY 3 YEARS OLD!
© 2002 Ripley Entertainment Inc.
Dist. by United Feature Syndicate, Inc.
2-20
www.comics.com

24. Merrick was in fact exhibited in a closed wax museum owned by Tom Norman, and the waxworks did indeed have wax versions of some of Jack the Ripper's victims. As an interesting sidenote, some researchers have foolishly tried to connect Merrick to the Ripper slayings, despite the fact that his deformities made even walking – let along stalking and killing a grown woman – extremely difficult.

25. It was long thought that Merrick suffered from an extremely advanced or severe case of elephantiasis, which causes thickening of the skin and swelling of limbs. However, it's now widely believed that Merrick was afflicted with Proteus Syndrome, an extremely rare disease identified in 1979.

26. Merrick was not, in fact, mentally handicapped in any way. He just had difficult speaking due to his deformities.

27. In June of 1886, an Austrian promoter (who was not associated with Tom Norman in any way) robbed Merrick and left him stranded in Brussels, Belgium.

28. When Merrick returned from Austria, he was admitted to the London Hospital to be treated for bronchitis, malnutrition, and exhaustion.

29. In 1888, Joseph made a cardboard church for a stage actress named Madge Kendall. He hoped to meet Kendall when he presented her with the church, but she sent her husband to receive the gift instead.

30. Contrary to popular belief, the Elephant Man's skeleton is not in the hands of a "private collector." In reality, the London Hospital has retained Merrick's remains since his death.

31. If drinking whiskey was Chang's vice, then playing poker was Eng's.

32. It's believed that Chang died from a blood clot in his brain.

33. This may be the most accurate theory, actually. It's believed that Chang and Eng shared some vascular connections between their livers, and possibly an artery. However, many surgeons believe that they could be safely separated if born today.

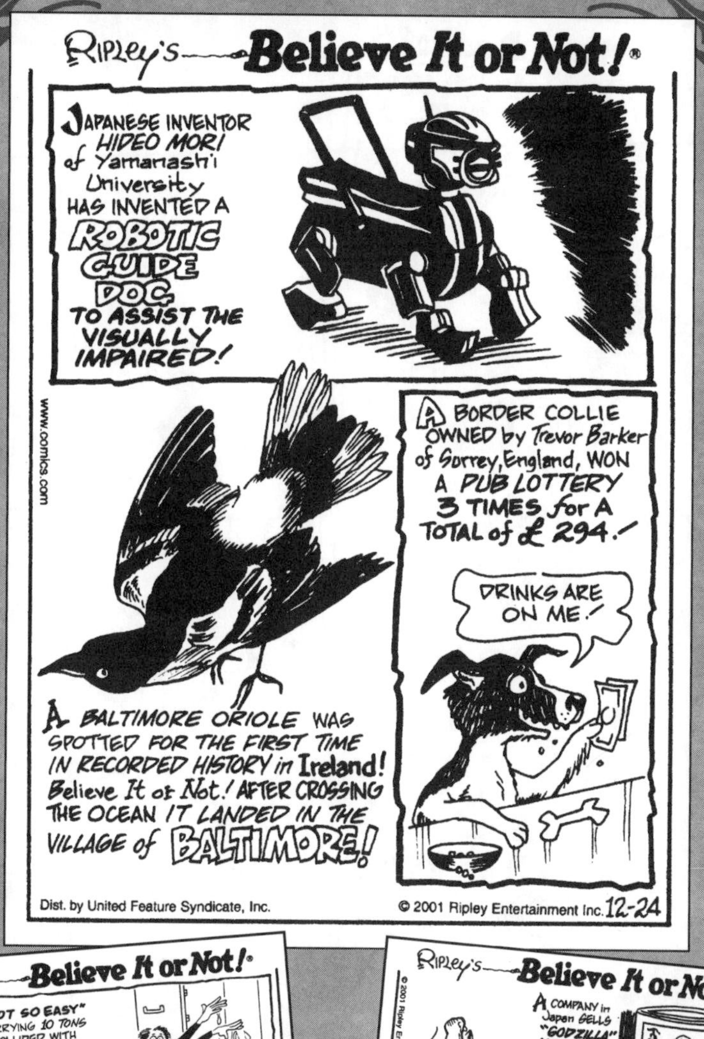
Ripley's Believe It or Not!®
JAPANESE INVENTOR HIDEO MORI of Yamanashi University HAS INVENTED A ROBOTIC GUIDE DOG TO ASSIST THE VISUALLY IMPAIRED!
www.comics.com
A BORDER COLLIE OWNED by Trevor Barker of Sorrey, England, WON A PUB LOTTERY 3 TIMES for A TOTAL of £ 294.!
DRINKS ARE ON ME!
A BALTIMORE ORIOLE WAS SPOTTED FOR THE FIRST TIME IN RECORDED HISTORY in Ireland! Believe It or Not! AFTER CROSSING THE OCEAN IT LANDED IN THE VILLAGE of BALTIMORE!
Dist. by United Feature Syndicate, Inc.
© 2001 Ripley Entertainment Inc. 12-24

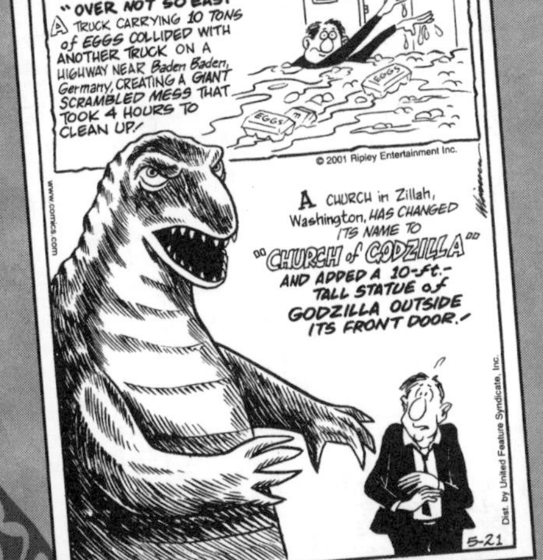
Ripley's Believe It or Not!®
"OVER NOT SO EASY"
A TRUCK CARRYING 10 TONS of EGGS COLLIDED WITH ANOTHER TRUCK ON A HIGHWAY NEAR Baden Baden, Germany, CREATING A GIANT SCRAMBLED MESS THAT TOOK 4 HOURS TO CLEAN UP!
EGGS
© 2001 Ripley Entertainment Inc.
www.comics.com
A CHURCH in Zillah, Washington, HAS CHANGED ITS NAME TO "CHURCH of GODZILLA" AND ADDED A 10-ft.-TALL STATUE of GODZILLA OUTSIDE ITS FRONT DOOR.!
Dist. by United Feature Syndicate, Inc.
5-21

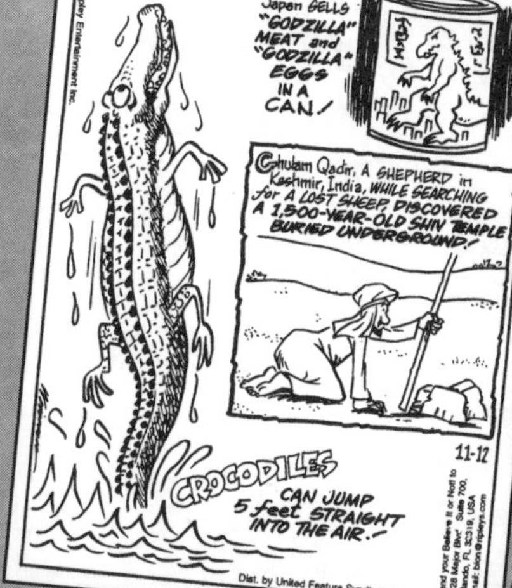
Ripley's Believe It or Not!®
© 2001 Ripley Entertainment Inc.
A COMPANY in Japan SELLS "GODZILLA" MEAT and "GODZILLA" EGGS IN A CAN!
Ghulam Qadir, A SHEPHERD in Kashmir, India, WHILE SEARCHING for A LOST SHEEP, DISCOVERED A 1,500-YEAR-OLD SHIV TEMPLE BURIED UNDERGROUND!
11-12
CROCODILES CAN JUMP 5 feet STRAIGHT INTO THE AIR!
Dist. by United Feature Syndicate, Inc.
Send your Believe It or Not! to 5728 Major Blvd. Suite 700, Orlando, FL 32319, USA
e-mail: bion@ripleys.com

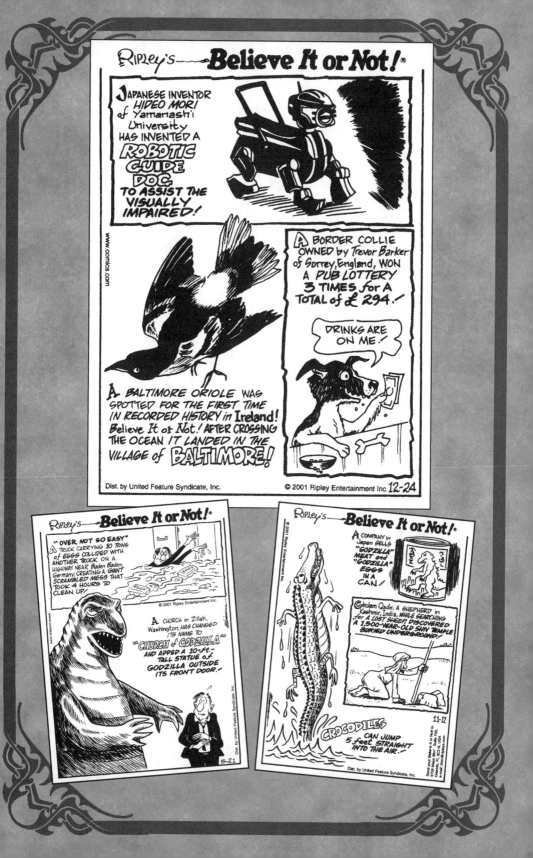

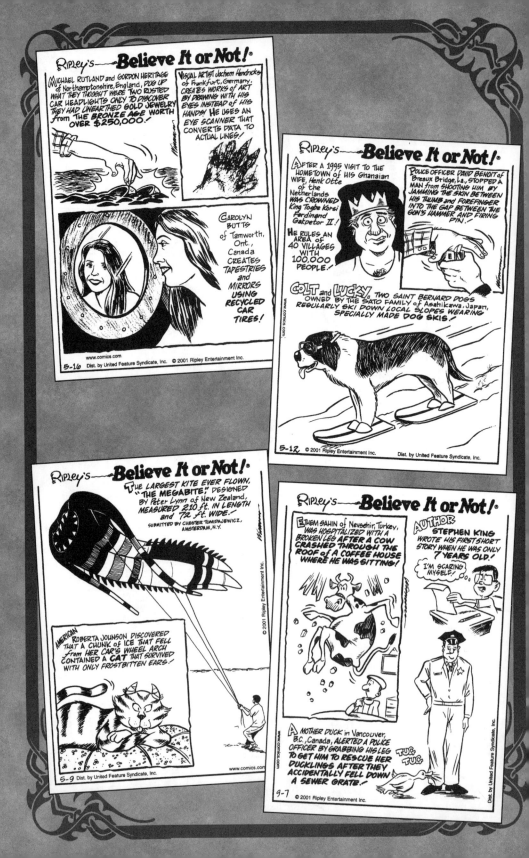

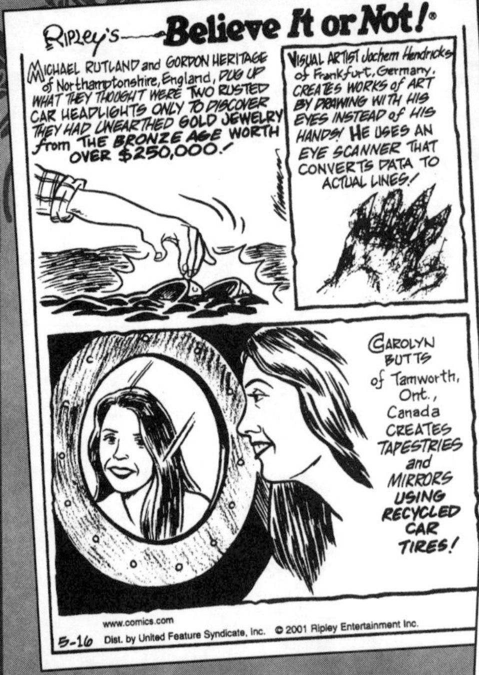
Ripley's Believe It or Not!
MICHAEL RUTLAND and GORDON HERITAGE of Northamptonshire, England, DUG UP WHAT THEY THOUGHT WERE TWO RUSTED CAR HEADLIGHTS ONLY TO DISCOVER THEY HAD UNEARTHED GOLD JEWELRY from THE BRONZE AGE WORTH OVER $250,000.!
VISUAL ARTIST Jochem Hendricks of Frankfurt, Germany, CREATES WORKS of ART BY DRAWING WITH HIS EYES INSTEAD of HIS HANDS! HE USES AN EYE SCANNER THAT CONVERTS DATA TO ACTUAL LINES!
CAROLYN BUTTS of Tamworth, Ont., Canada CREATES TAPESTRIES and MIRRORS USING RECYCLED CAR TIRES!
www.comics.com
5-16 Dist. by United Feature Syndicate, Inc. © 2001 Ripley Entertainment Inc.

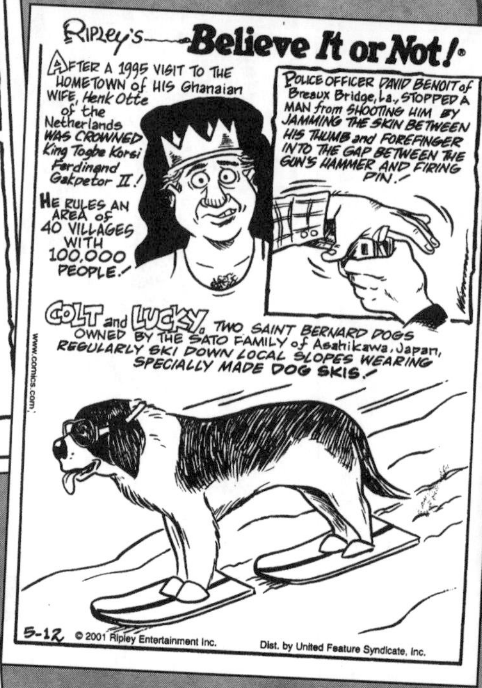
Ripley's Believe It or Not!
AFTER A 1995 VISIT TO THE HOMETOWN of HIS Ghanaian WIFE, Henk Otte of the Netherlands WAS CROWNED King Togbe Korsi Ferdinand Gakpetor II!
HE RULES AN AREA of 40 VILLAGES WITH 100,000 PEOPLE.!
POLICE OFFICER DAVID BENOIT of Breaux Bridge, La., STOPPED A MAN from SHOOTING HIM BY JAMMING THE SKIN BETWEEN HIS THUMB and FOREFINGER INTO THE GAP BETWEEN THE GUN'S HAMMER AND FIRING PIN.!
COLT and LUCKY, TWO SAINT BERNARD DOGS OWNED BY THE SATO FAMILY of Asahikawa, Japan, REGULARLY SKI DOWN LOCAL SLOPES WEARING SPECIALLY MADE DOG SKIS.!
www.comics.com
5-12 © 2001 Ripley Entertainment Inc. Dist. by United Feature Syndicate, Inc.

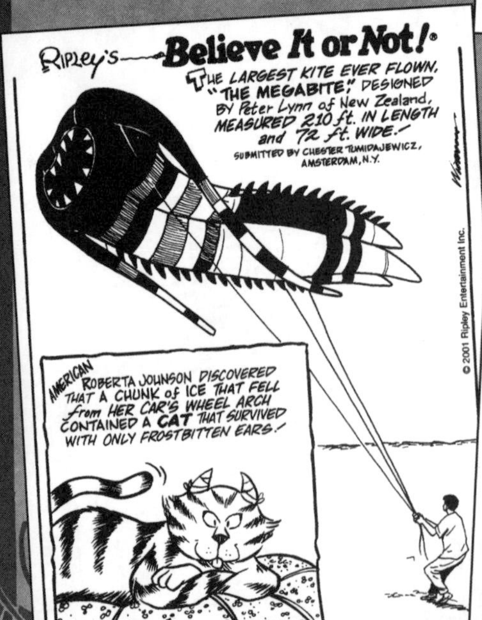
Ripley's Believe It or Not!
THE LARGEST KITE EVER FLOWN, "THE MEGABITE," DESIGNED BY Peter Lynn of New Zealand, MEASURED 210 ft. IN LENGTH and 72 ft. WIDE.!
SUBMITTED BY CHESTER TUMIDAJEWICZ, AMSTERDAM, N.Y.
AMERICAN ROBERTA JOHNSON DISCOVERED THAT A CHUNK of ICE THAT FELL from HER CAR'S WHEEL ARCH CONTAINED A CAT THAT SURVIVED WITH ONLY FROSTBITTEN EARS!
© 2001 Ripley Entertainment Inc.
www.comics.com
5-9 Dist. by United Feature Syndicate, Inc.

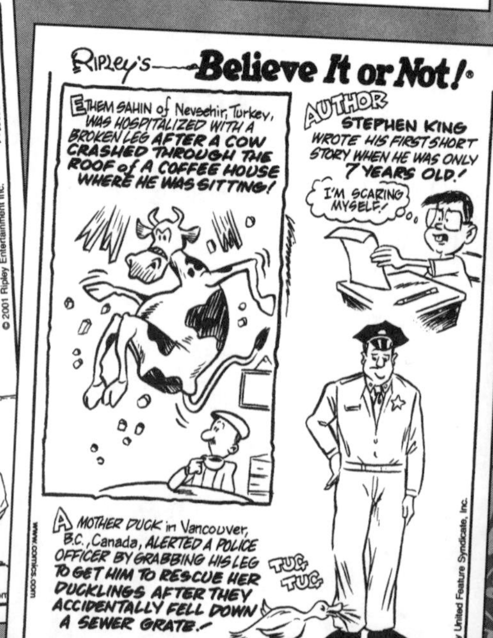
Ripley's Believe It or Not!
ETHEM SAHIN of Nevsehir, Turkey, WAS HOSPITALIZED WITH A BROKEN LEG AFTER A COW CRASHED THROUGH THE ROOF of A COFFEE HOUSE WHERE HE WAS SITTING!
AUTHOR STEPHEN KING WROTE HIS FIRST SHORT STORY WHEN HE WAS ONLY 7 YEARS OLD.!
I'M SCARING MYSELF!
A MOTHER DUCK in Vancouver, B.C., Canada, ALERTED A POLICE OFFICER BY GRABBING HIS LEG TO GET HIM TO RESCUE HER DUCKLINGS AFTER THEY ACCIDENTALLY FELL DOWN A SEWER GRATE.!
TUG TUG
www.comics.com
9-7 © 2001 Ripley Entertainment Inc.
Dist. by United Feature Syndicate, Inc.

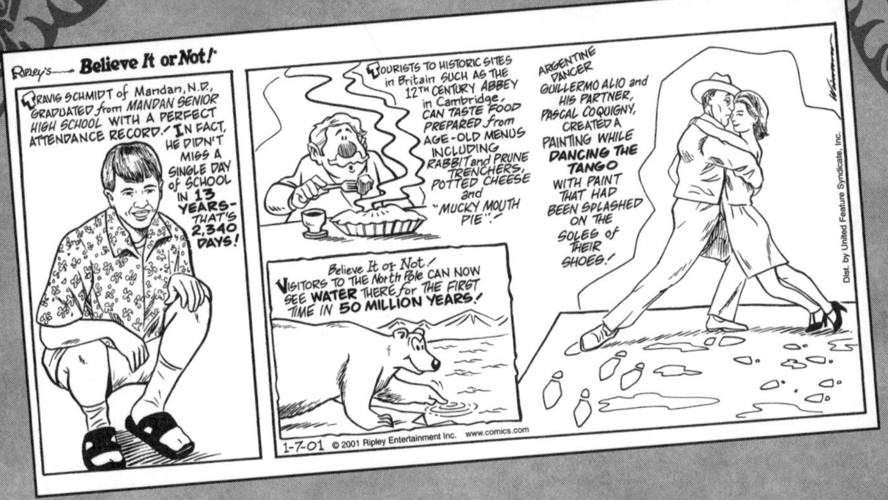

Ripley's Believe It or Not!
Travis Schmidt of Mandan, N.D., graduated from Mandan Senior High School with a perfect attendance record! In fact, he didn't miss a single day of school in 13 years - that's 2,340 days!
Tourists to historic sites in Britain such as the 12th century abbey in Cambridge, can taste food prepared from age-old menus including rabbit and prune trenchers, potted cheese and "Mucky Mouth Pie"!
Believe It or Not! Visitors to the North Pole can now see water there for the first time in 50 million years!
Argentine dancer Guillermo Alio and his partner, Pascal Coquigny, created a painting while dancing the tango with paint that had been splashed on the soles of their shoes!
Dist. by United Feature Syndicate, Inc.
1-7-01 © 2001 Ripley Entertainment Inc. www.comics.com

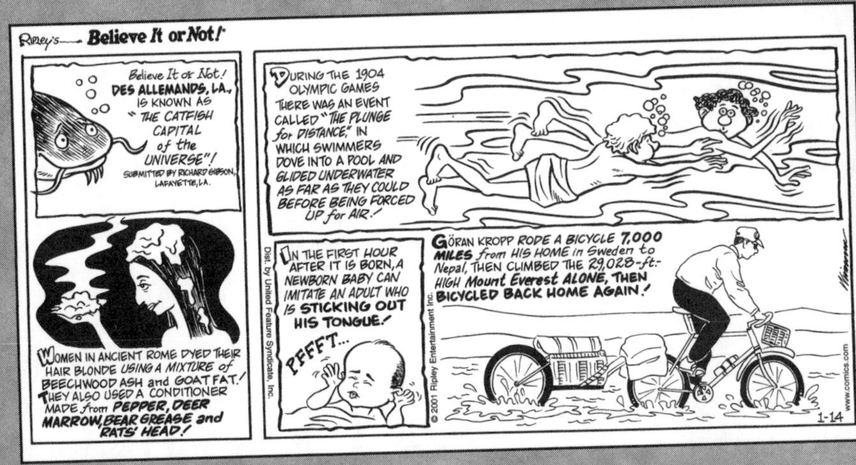

Ripley's Believe It or Not!
Believe It or Not! Des Allemands, La., is known as "The Catfish Capital of the Universe"!
Submitted by Richard Gibson, Lafayette, La.
During the 1904 Olympic Games there was an event called "The Plunge for Distance," in which swimmers dove into a pool and glided underwater as far as they could before being forced up for air!
Women in ancient Rome dyed their hair blonde using a mixture of beechwood ash and goat fat! They also used a conditioner made from pepper, deer marrow, bear grease and rats' head!
In the first hour after it is born, a newborn baby can imitate an adult who is sticking out his tongue!
PFFFT...
Göran Kropp rode a bicycle 7,000 miles from his home in Sweden to Nepal, then climbed the 29,028-ft.-high Mount Everest alone, then bicycled back home again!
Dist. by United Feature Syndicate, Inc.
© 2001 Ripley Entertainment Inc.
www.comics.com
1-14

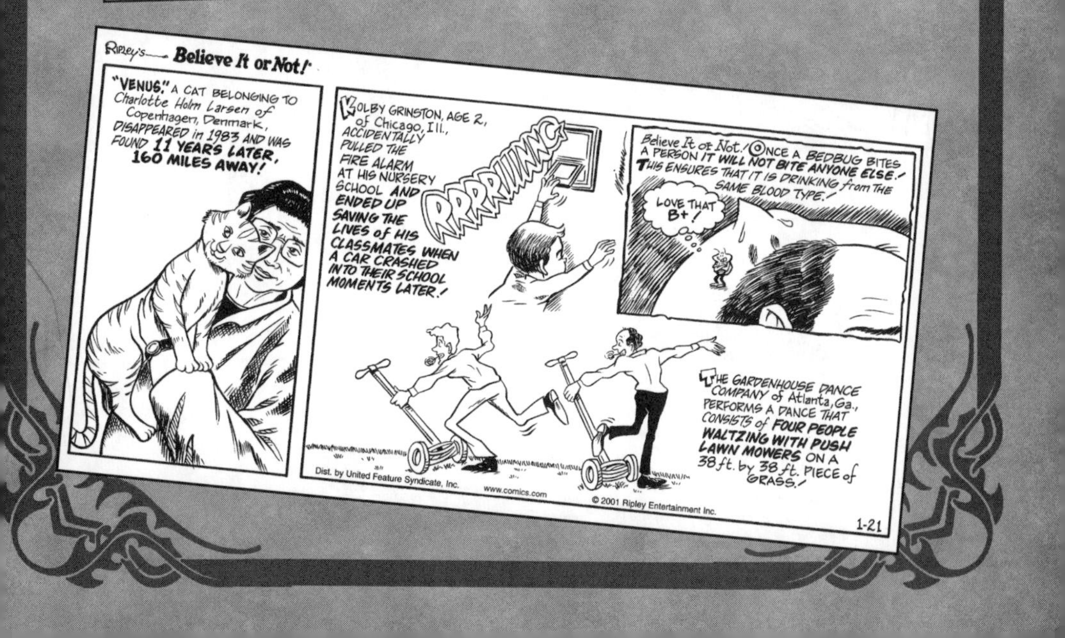

Ripley's Believe It or Not!
"Venus," a cat belonging to Charlotte Holm Larsen of Copenhagen, Denmark, disappeared in 1983 and was found 11 years later, 160 miles away!
Kolby Grinston, age 2, of Chicago, Ill., accidentally pulled the fire alarm at his nursery school and ended up saving the lives of his classmates when a car crashed into their school moments later!
RRRRIIINNG
Believe It or Not! Once a bedbug bites a person it will not bite anyone else! This ensures that it is drinking from the same blood type!
Love that B+!
The Gardenhouse Dance Company of Atlanta, Ga., performs a dance that consists of four people waltzing with push lawn mowers on a 38 ft. by 38 ft. piece of grass!
Dist. by United Feature Syndicate, Inc. www.comics.com © 2001 Ripley Entertainment Inc.
1-21

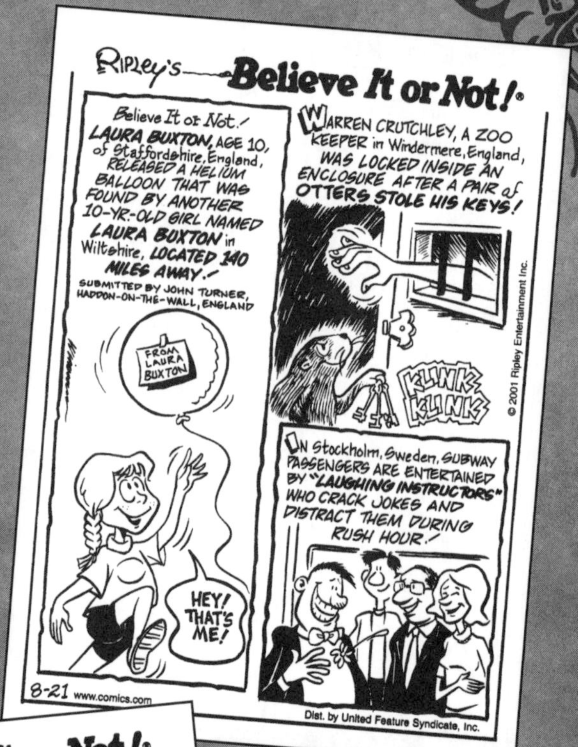

Ripley's Believe It or Not!
Believe It or Not!
LAURA BUXTON, AGE 10, of Staffordshire, England, RELEASED A HELIUM BALLOON THAT WAS FOUND BY ANOTHER 10-YR.-OLD GIRL NAMED LAURA BUXTON in Wiltshire, LOCATED 140 MILES AWAY!
SUBMITTED BY JOHN TURNER, HADDON-ON-THE-WALL, ENGLAND
FROM LAURA BUXTON
HEY! THAT'S ME!
WARREN CRUTCHLEY, A ZOO KEEPER in Windermere, England, WAS LOCKED INSIDE AN ENCLOSURE AFTER A PAIR of OTTERS STOLE HIS KEYS!
KLINK KLINK
© 2001 Ripley Entertainment Inc.
IN Stockholm, Sweden, SUBWAY PASSENGERS ARE ENTERTAINED BY "LAUGHING INSTRUCTORS" WHO CRACK JOKES AND DISTRACT THEM DURING RUSH HOUR!
8-21 www.comics.com
Dist. by United Feature Syndicate, Inc.

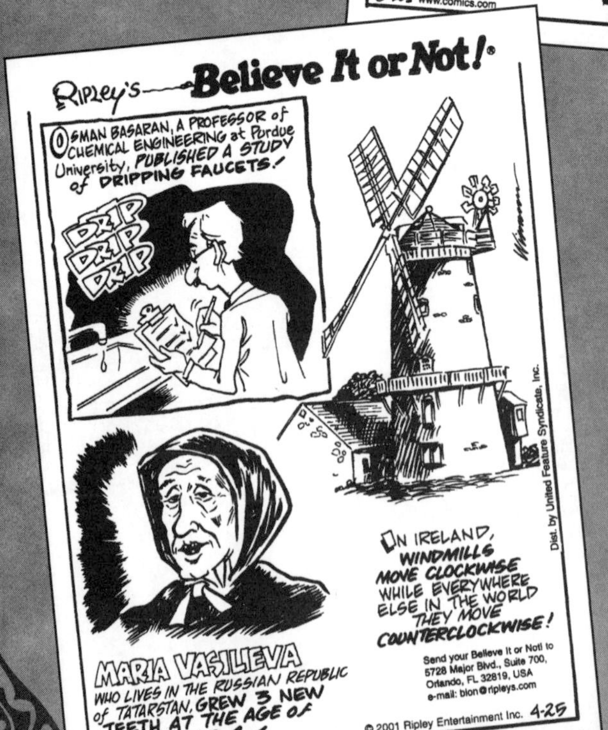

Ripley's Believe It or Not!
OSMAN BASARAN, A PROFESSOR of CHEMICAL ENGINEERING at Purdue University, PUBLISHED A STUDY of DRIPPING FAUCETS!
DRIP DRIP DRIP
MARIA VASILIEVA
WHO LIVES IN THE RUSSIAN REPUBLIC of TATARSTAN, GREW 3 NEW TEETH AT THE AGE of 104!
IN IRELAND, WINDMILLS MOVE CLOCKWISE WHILE EVERYWHERE ELSE IN THE WORLD THEY MOVE COUNTERCLOCKWISE!
Dist. by United Feature Syndicate, Inc.
Send your Believe It or Not! to 5728 Major Blvd., Suite 700, Orlando, FL 32819, USA
e-mail: bion@ripleys.com
© 2001 Ripley Entertainment Inc. 4-25

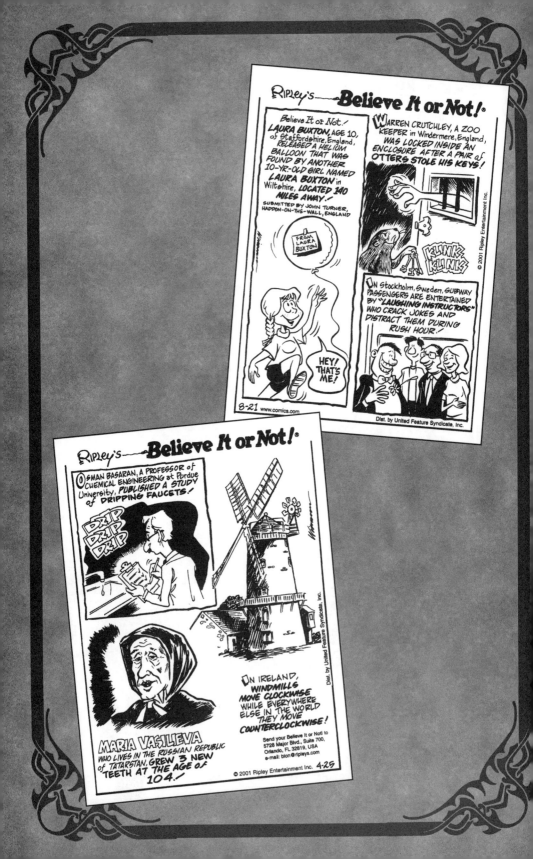

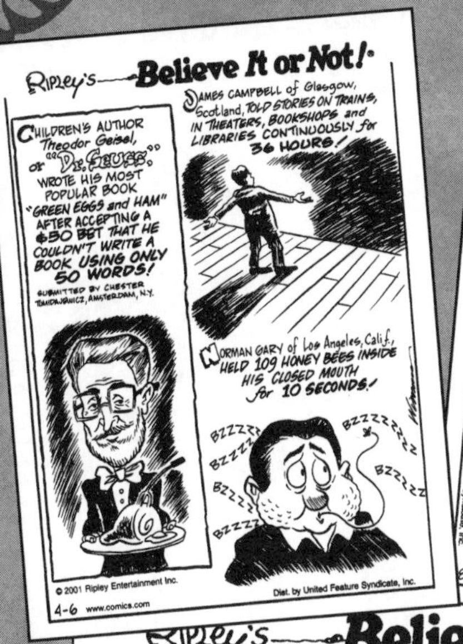
Ripley's Believe It or Not!®
CHILDREN'S AUTHOR Theodor Geisel, or "DR. SEUSS," WROTE HIS MOST POPULAR BOOK "GREEN EGGS and HAM" AFTER ACCEPTING A $50 BET THAT HE COULDN'T WRITE A BOOK USING ONLY 50 WORDS!
SUBMITTED BY CHESTER TOMIDAJEWICZ, AMSTERDAM, N.Y.
JAMES CAMPBELL of Glasgow, Scotland, TOLD STORIES ON TRAINS, IN THEATERS, BOOKSHOPS and LIBRARIES CONTINUOUSLY for 36 HOURS!
NORMAN GARY of Los Angeles, Calif., HELD 109 HONEY BEES INSIDE HIS CLOSED MOUTH for 10 SECONDS!
BZZZZ
© 2001 Ripley Entertainment Inc.
Dist. by United Feature Syndicate, Inc.
4-6 www.comics.com

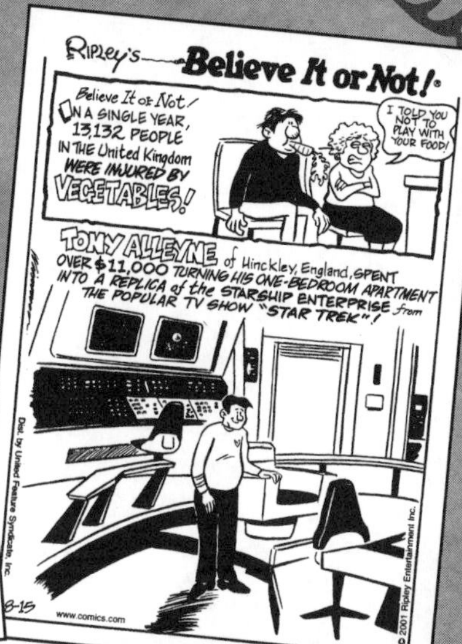
Ripley's Believe It or Not!®
Believe It or Not! IN A SINGLE YEAR, 13,132 PEOPLE IN THE United Kingdom WERE INJURED BY VEGETABLES!
I TOLD YOU NOT TO PLAY WITH YOUR FOOD!
TONY ALLEYNE of Hinckley, England, SPENT OVER $11,000 TURNING HIS ONE-BEDROOM APARTMENT INTO A REPLICA of the STARSHIP ENTERPRISE from THE POPULAR TV SHOW "STAR TREK"!
Dist. by United Feature Syndicate, Inc.
© 2001 Ripley Entertainment Inc.
8-15 www.comics.com

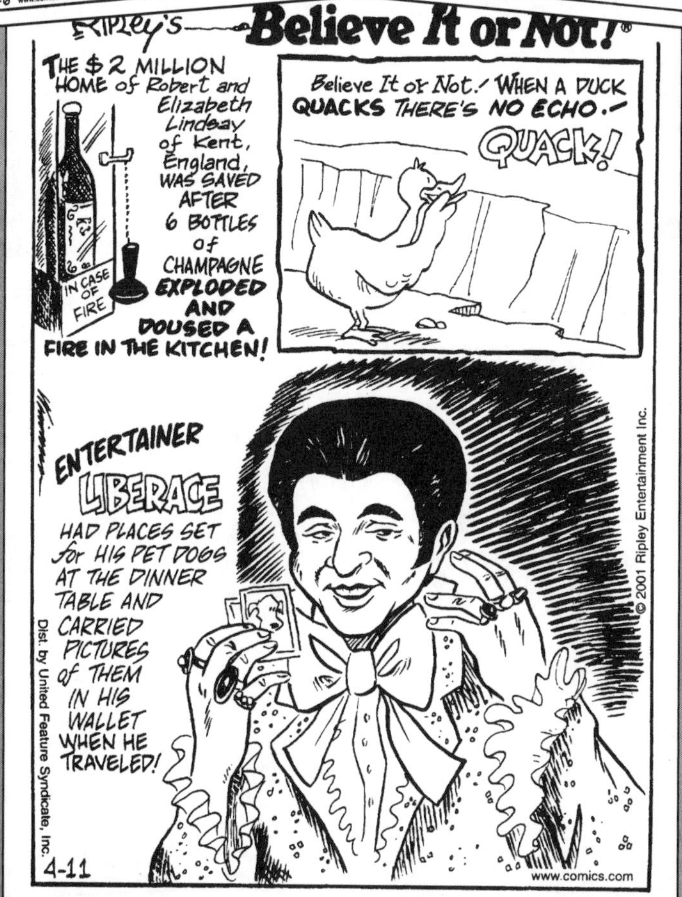
Ripley's Believe It or Not!®
THE $2 MILLION HOME of Robert and Elizabeth Lindsay of Kent, England, WAS SAVED AFTER 6 BOTTLES of CHAMPAGNE EXPLODED AND DOUSED A FIRE IN THE KITCHEN!
IN CASE OF FIRE
Believe It or Not! WHEN A DUCK QUACKS THERE'S NO ECHO!
QUACK!
ENTERTAINER LIBERACE HAD PLACES SET for HIS PET DOGS AT THE DINNER TABLE AND CARRIED PICTURES of THEM IN HIS WALLET WHEN HE TRAVELED!
© 2001 Ripley Entertainment Inc.
Dist. by United Feature Syndicate, Inc.
4-11
www.comics.com

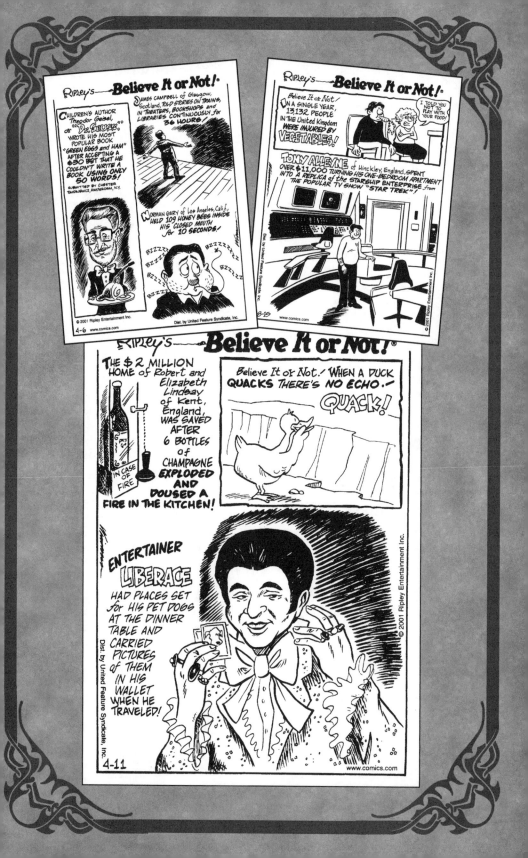

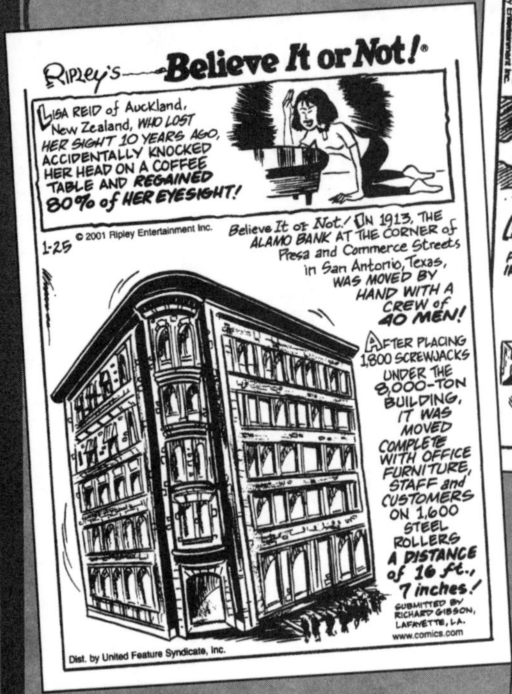
Ripley's Believe It or Not!
LISA REID of Auckland, New Zealand, WHO LOST HER SIGHT 10 YEARS AGO, ACCIDENTALLY KNOCKED HER HEAD ON A COFFEE TABLE AND REGAINED 80% of HER EYESIGHT!
1-25
© 2001 Ripley Entertainment Inc.
Believe It or Not! IN 1913, THE ALAMO BANK AT THE CORNER of Presa and Commerce Streets in San Antonio, Texas, WAS MOVED BY HAND WITH A CREW of 40 MEN!
AFTER PLACING 1,800 SCREWJACKS UNDER THE 8,000-TON BUILDING, IT WAS MOVED COMPLETE WITH OFFICE FURNITURE, STAFF and CUSTOMERS ON 1,600 STEEL ROLLERS A DISTANCE of 16 ft., 7 inches!
SUBMITTED BY RICHARD GIBSON, LAFAYETTE, LA.
www.comics.com
Dist. by United Feature Syndicate, Inc.

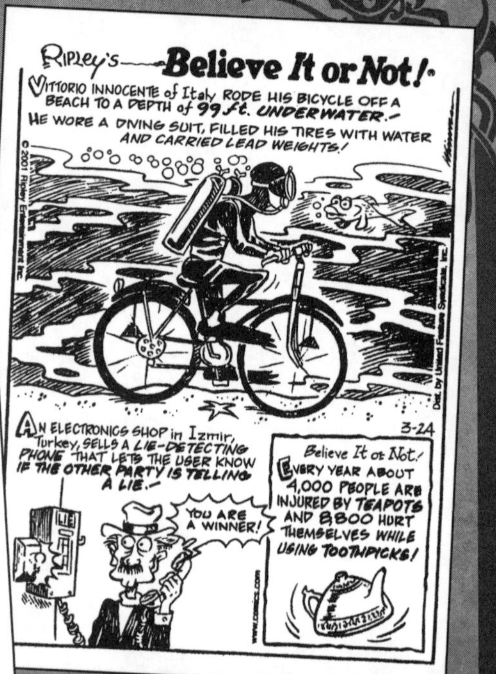
Ripley's Believe It or Not!
VITTORIO INNOCENTE of Italy RODE HIS BICYCLE OFF A BEACH TO A DEPTH of 99 ft. UNDERWATER.–
HE WORE A DIVING SUIT, FILLED HIS TIRES WITH WATER AND CARRIED LEAD WEIGHTS!
© 2001 Ripley Entertainment Inc.
Dist. by United Feature Syndicate, Inc.
3-24
AN ELECTRONICS SHOP in Izmir, Turkey, SELLS A LIE-DETECTING PHONE THAT LETS THE USER KNOW IF THE OTHER PARTY IS TELLING A LIE.–
LIE
YOU ARE A WINNER!
Believe It or Not! EVERY YEAR ABOUT 4,000 PEOPLE ARE INJURED BY TEAPOTS AND 8,800 HURT THEMSELVES WHILE USING TOOTHPICKS!
www.comics.com

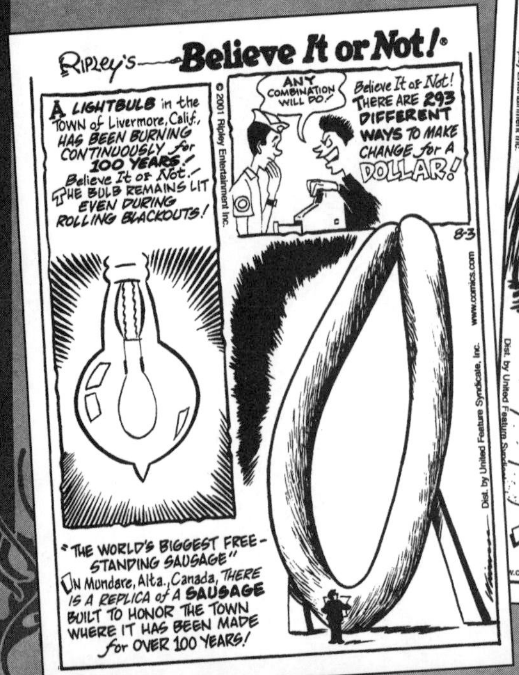
Ripley's Believe It or Not!
A LIGHTBULB in the TOWN of Livermore, Calif., HAS BEEN BURNING CONTINUOUSLY for 100 YEARS!– Believe It or Not.– THE BULB REMAINS LIT EVEN DURING ROLLING BLACKOUTS!
© 2001 Ripley Entertainment Inc.
ANY COMBINATION WILL DO!
Believe It or Not! THERE ARE 293 DIFFERENT WAYS TO MAKE CHANGE for A DOLLAR!
8-3
www.comics.com
Dist. by United Feature Syndicate, Inc.
"THE WORLD'S BIGGEST FREE-STANDING SAUSAGE"
IN Mundare, Alta., Canada, THERE IS A REPLICA of A SAUSAGE BUILT TO HONOR THE TOWN WHERE IT HAS BEEN MADE for OVER 100 YEARS!

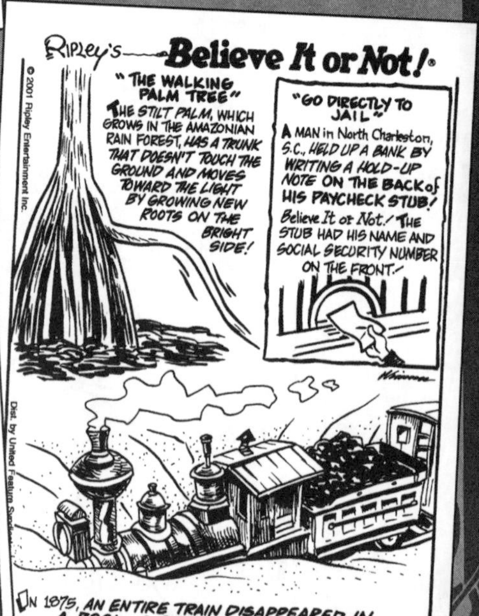
Ripley's Believe It or Not!
© 2001 Ripley Entertainment Inc.
"THE WALKING PALM TREE"
THE STILT PALM, WHICH GROWS IN THE AMAZONIAN RAIN FOREST, HAS A TRUNK THAT DOESN'T TOUCH THE GROUND AND MOVES TOWARD THE LIGHT BY GROWING NEW ROOTS ON THE BRIGHT SIDE!
"GO DIRECTLY TO JAIL"
A MAN in North Charleston, S.C., HELD UP A BANK BY WRITING A HOLD-UP NOTE ON THE BACK of HIS PAYCHECK STUB! Believe It or Not! THE STUB HAD HIS NAME AND SOCIAL SECURITY NUMBER ON THE FRONT.–
Dist. by United Feature Syndicate, Inc.
IN 1875, AN ENTIRE TRAIN DISAPPEARED IN A POOL of QUICKSAND in Colorado.–
www.comics.com
SUBMITTED BY RICHARD GIBSON, LAFAYETTE, LA
2-22

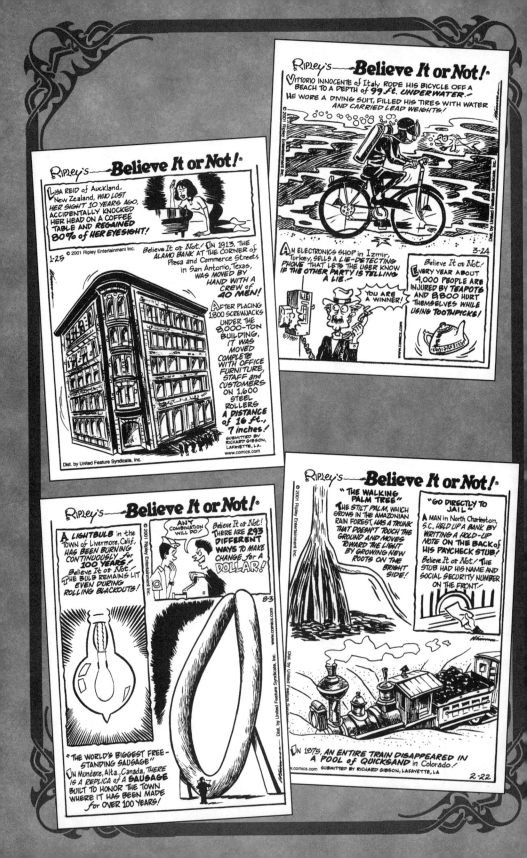

Ripley's Believe It or Not!®
The government of India has placed several large monkeys on its payroll!
The animals were hired to scare away thousands of smaller rhesus monkeys who have been attacking government workers and wrecking offices!
The average human body contains enough carbon to make 900 pencils!
Mahammed Sabir Sipra of Pakistan can lift 3.1 lbs. using his eyelids and can lift 68.2 lbs. with his teeth!
Dist. by United Feature Syndicate, Inc.
6-25
© 2001 Ripley Entertainment Inc.

Ripley's Believe It or Not!®
Believe It or Not!
There are 336 dimples in a regulation-size golf ball!
An oak tree does not produce acorns until it is 50 years old!
Charles Webb, author of the the bestselling novel "The Graduate," signed away the royalties from the book to his favorite charity and chose to work at a variety of jobs — including fruit picker — rather than accumulate any wealth!
Who needs fame and fortune?!
www.comics.com
7-19 © 2001 Ripley Entertainment Inc.
Dist. by United Feature Syndicate, Inc.

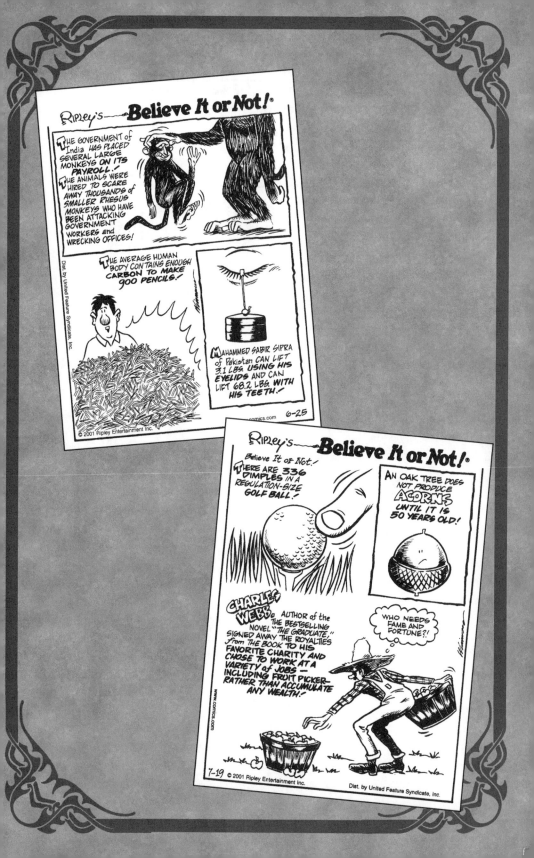

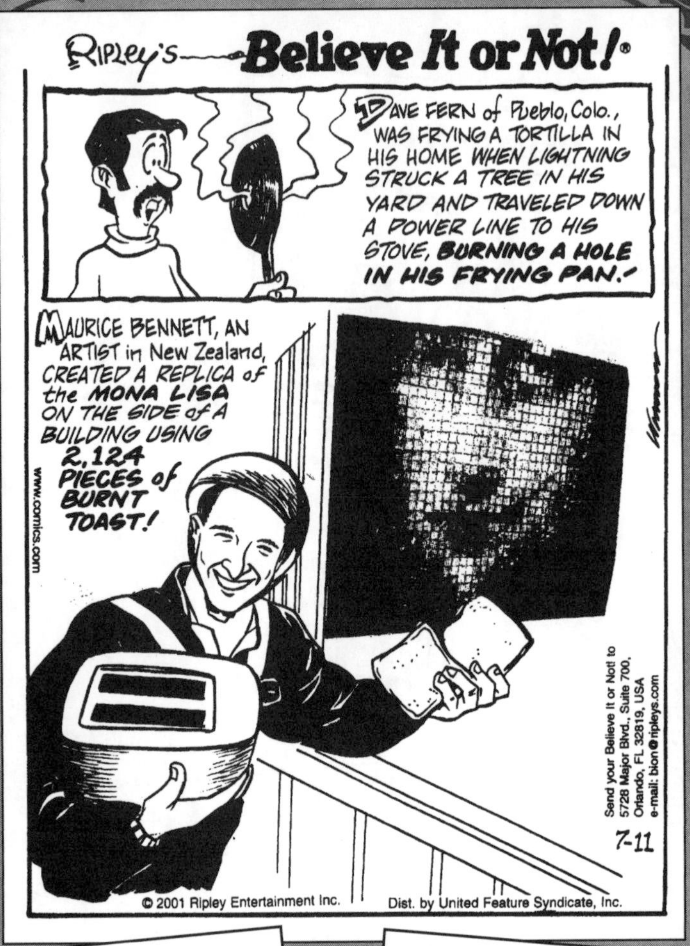
Ripley's Believe It or Not!®
DAVE FERN of Pueblo, Colo., WAS FRYING A TORTILLA IN HIS HOME WHEN LIGHTNING STRUCK A TREE IN HIS YARD AND TRAVELED DOWN A POWER LINE TO HIS STOVE, BURNING A HOLE IN HIS FRYING PAN.!
MAURICE BENNETT, AN ARTIST in New Zealand, CREATED A REPLICA of the MONA LISA ON THE SIDE of A BUILDING USING 2,124 PIECES of BURNT TOAST!
www.comics.com
Send your Believe It or Not! to 5728 Major Blvd., Suite 700, Orlando, FL 32819, USA e-mail: bion@ripleys.com
7-11
© 2001 Ripley Entertainment Inc.
Dist. by United Feature Syndicate, Inc.

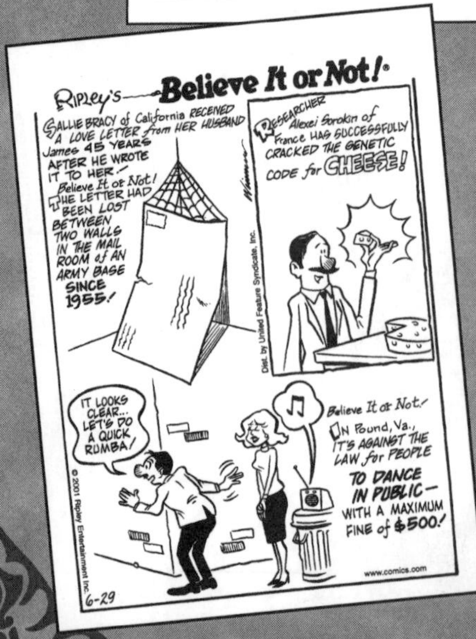
Ripley's Believe It or Not!®
SALLIE BRACY of California RECEIVED A LOVE LETTER from HER HUSBAND James 45 YEARS AFTER HE WROTE IT TO HER.! Believe It or Not! THE LETTER HAD BEEN LOST BETWEEN TWO WALLS IN THE MAIL ROOM of AN ARMY BASE SINCE 1955!
RESEARCHER Alexei Sorokin of France HAS SUCCESSFULLY CRACKED THE GENETIC CODE for CHEESE!
Dist. by United Feature Syndicate, Inc.
IT LOOKS CLEAR... LET'S DO A QUICK RUMBA!
Believe It or Not! IN Pound, Va., IT'S AGAINST THE LAW for PEOPLE TO DANCE IN PUBLIC — WITH A MAXIMUM FINE of $500!
© 2001 Ripley Entertainment Inc.
www.comics.com
6-29

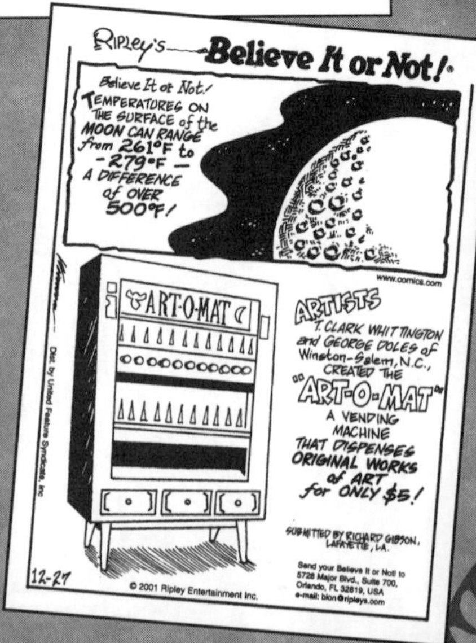
Ripley's Believe It or Not!®
Believe It or Not! TEMPERATURES ON THE SURFACE of the MOON CAN RANGE from 261°F to -279°F — A DIFFERENCE of OVER 500°F!
www.comics.com
ART-O-MAT
ARTISTS T. CLARK WHITTINGTON and GEORGE DOLES of Winston-Salem, N.C., CREATED THE "ART-O-MAT"® A VENDING MACHINE THAT DISPENSES ORIGINAL WORKS of ART for ONLY $5!
SUBMITTED BY RICHARD GIBSON, LAFAYETTE, LA.
Dist. by United Feature Syndicate, Inc.
12-27
© 2001 Ripley Entertainment Inc.
Send your Believe It or Not! to 5728 Major Blvd., Suite 700, Orlando, FL 32819, USA e-mail: bion@ripleys.com

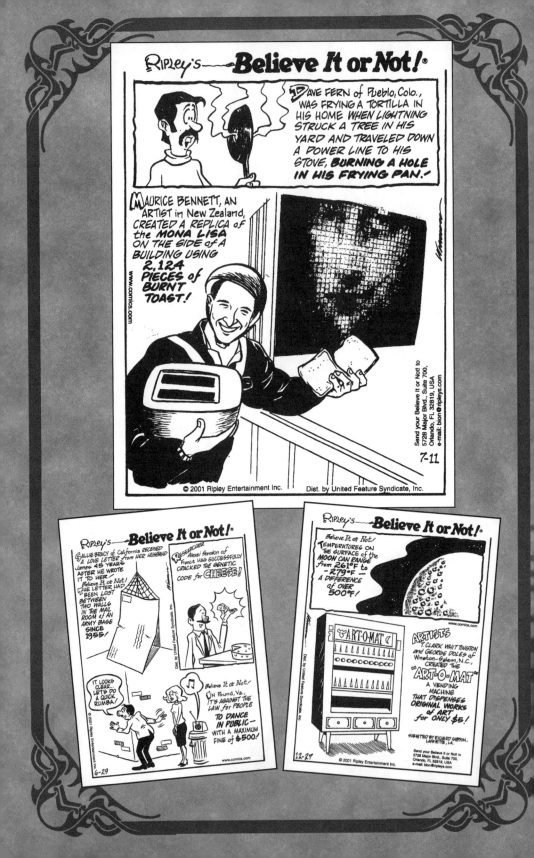

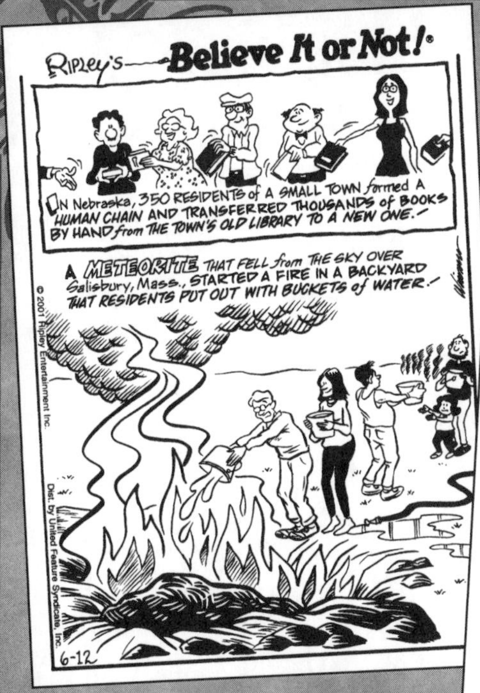

Ripley's Believe It or Not!®
IN Nebraska, 350 RESIDENTS of A SMALL TOWN formed A HUMAN CHAIN AND TRANSFERRED THOUSANDS of BOOKS BY HAND from THE TOWN'S OLD LIBRARY TO A NEW ONE.
A METEORITE THAT FELL from THE SKY OVER Salisbury, Mass., STARTED A FIRE IN A BACKYARD THAT RESIDENTS PUT OUT WITH BUCKETS of WATER.
© 2001 Ripley Entertainment Inc.
Dist. by United Feature Syndicate, Inc.
6-12

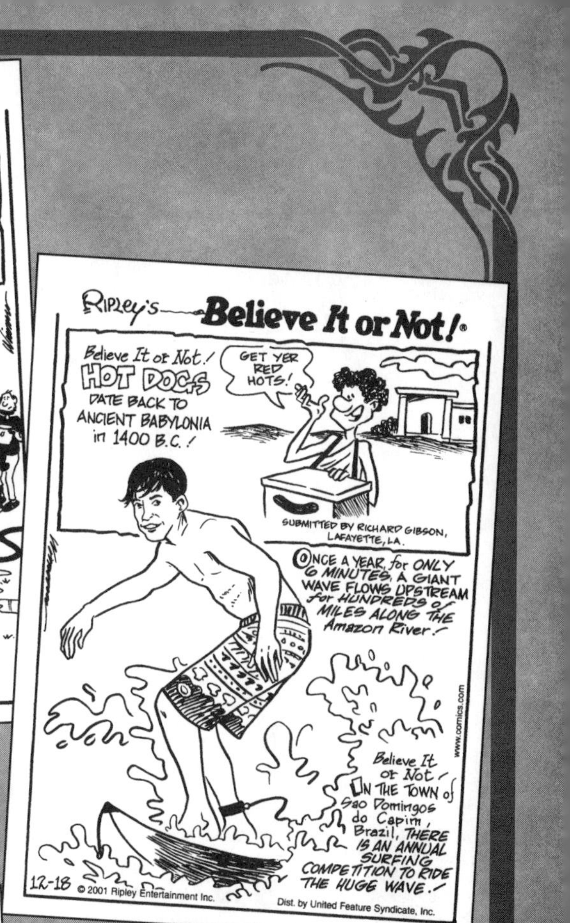

Ripley's Believe It or Not!®
Believe It or Not! HOT DOGS DATE BACK TO ANCIENT BABYLONIA in 1400 B.C.!
GET YER RED HOTS!
SUBMITTED BY RICHARD GIBSON, LAFAYETTE, LA.
ONCE A YEAR for ONLY 6 MINUTES, A GIANT WAVE FLOWS UPSTREAM for HUNDREDS of MILES ALONG THE Amazon River!
Believe It or Not! IN THE TOWN of Sao Domingos do Capim, Brazil, THERE IS AN ANNUAL SURFING COMPETITION TO RIDE THE HUGE WAVE.
www.comics.com
12-18 © 2001 Ripley Entertainment Inc.
Dist. by United Feature Syndicate, Inc.

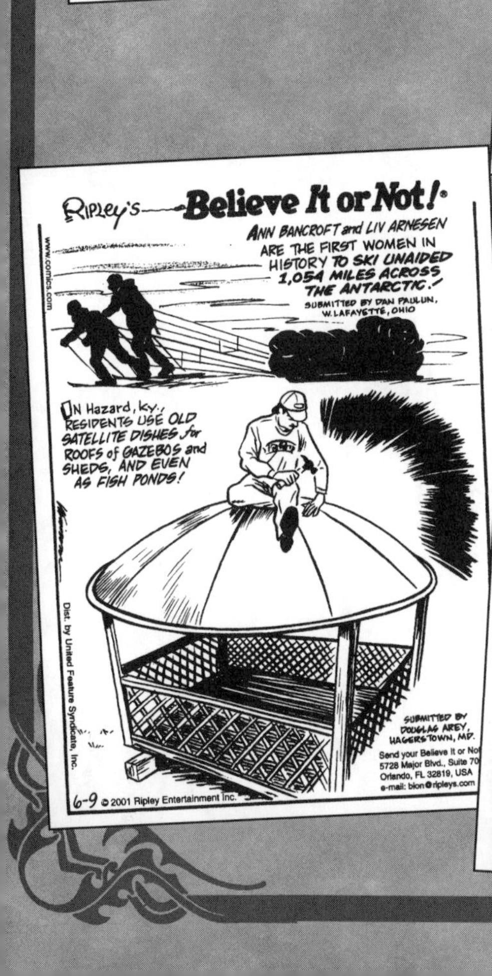

Ripley's Believe It or Not!®
ANN BANCROFT and LIV ARNESEN ARE THE FIRST WOMEN IN HISTORY TO SKI UNAIDED 1,054 MILES ACROSS THE ANTARCTIC.
SUBMITTED BY DAN PAULUN, W. LAFAYETTE, OHIO
www.comics.com
IN Hazard, Ky., RESIDENTS USE OLD SATELLITE DISHES for ROOFS of GAZEBOS and SHEDS, AND EVEN AS FISH PONDS!
SUBMITTED BY DOUGLAS AREY, HAGERSTOWN, MD.
Send your Believe It or Not
5728 Major Blvd., Suite 70
Orlando, FL 32819, USA
e-mail: bion@ripleys.com
Dist. by United Feature Syndicate, Inc.
6-9 © 2001 Ripley Entertainment Inc.

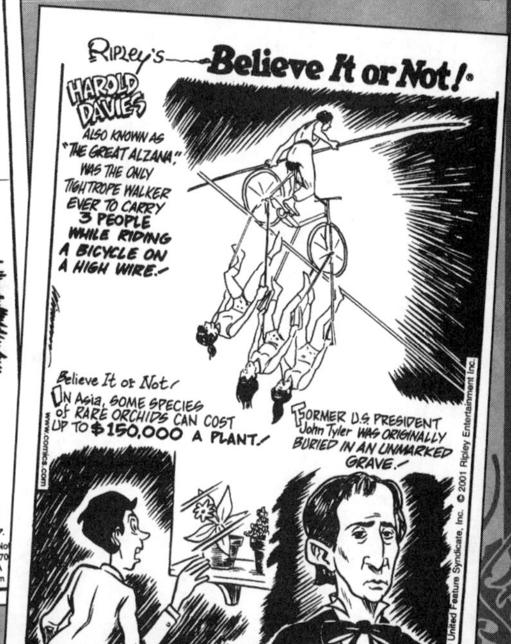

Ripley's Believe It or Not!®
HAROLD DAVIES ALSO KNOWN AS "THE GREAT ALZANA," WAS THE ONLY TIGHTROPE WALKER EVER TO CARRY 3 PEOPLE WHILE RIDING A BICYCLE ON A HIGH WIRE.
Believe It or Not! IN Asia, SOME SPECIES of RARE ORCHIDS CAN COST UP TO $150,000 A PLANT.
FORMER U.S. PRESIDENT John Tyler WAS ORIGINALLY BURIED IN AN UNMARKED GRAVE.
www.comics.com
Dist. by United Feature Syndicate, Inc. © 2001 Ripley Entertainment Inc.
6-4

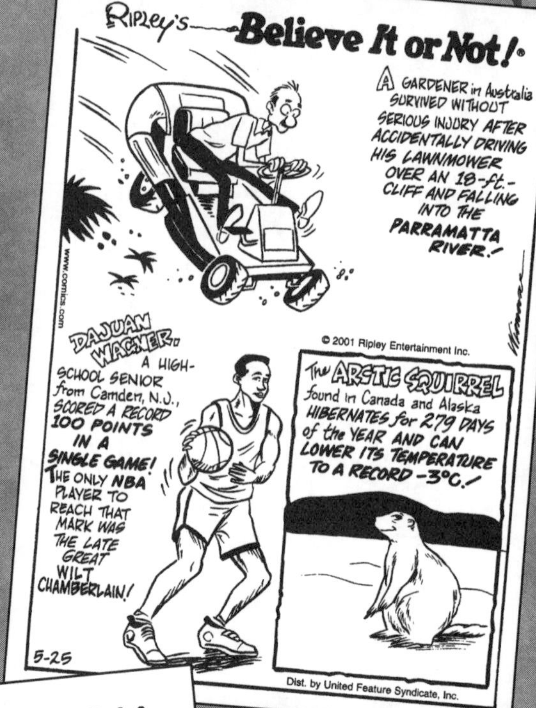
Ripley's Believe It or Not!®
A GARDENER in Australia SURVIVED WITHOUT SERIOUS INJURY AFTER ACCIDENTALLY DRIVING HIS LAWNMOWER OVER AN 18-ft.-CLIFF AND FALLING INTO THE PARRAMATTA RIVER!
www.comics.com
© 2001 Ripley Entertainment Inc.
DAJUAN WAGNER, A HIGH-SCHOOL SENIOR from Camden, N.J., SCORED A RECORD 100 POINTS IN A SINGLE GAME! THE ONLY NBA PLAYER TO REACH THAT MARK WAS THE LATE GREAT WILT CHAMBERLAIN!
The ARCTIC SQUIRREL found in Canada and Alaska HIBERNATES for 279 DAYS of the YEAR AND CAN LOWER ITS TEMPERATURE TO A RECORD -3°C.!
5-25
Dist. by United Feature Syndicate, Inc.

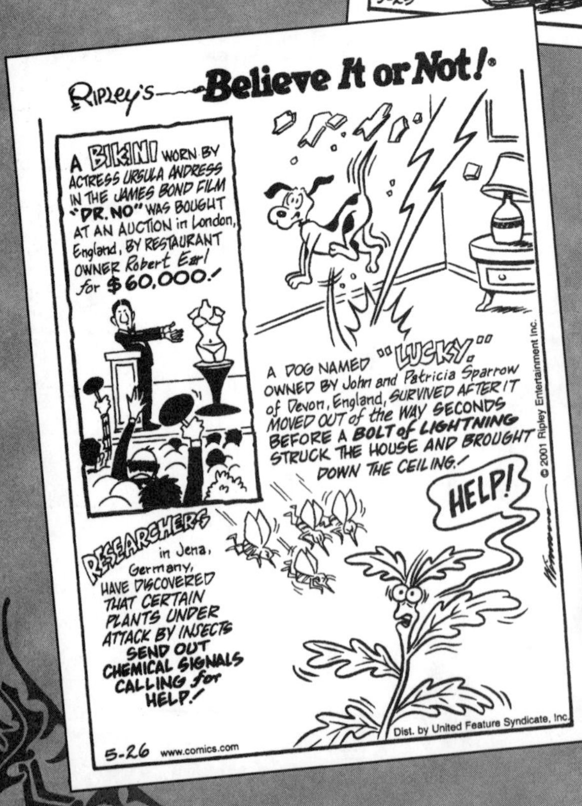
Ripley's Believe It or Not!®
A BIKINI WORN BY ACTRESS URSULA ANDRESS IN THE JAMES BOND FILM "DR. NO" WAS BOUGHT AT AN AUCTION in London, England, BY RESTAURANT OWNER Robert Earl for $60,000.!
A DOG NAMED "LUCKY," OWNED BY John and Patricia Sparrow of Devon, England, SURVIVED AFTER IT MOVED OUT of the WAY SECONDS BEFORE A BOLT of LIGHTNING STRUCK THE HOUSE AND BROUGHT DOWN THE CEILING!
© 2001 Ripley Entertainment Inc.
HELP!
RESEARCHERS in Jena, Germany, HAVE DISCOVERED THAT CERTAIN PLANTS UNDER ATTACK BY INSECTS SEND OUT CHEMICAL SIGNALS CALLING for HELP!
Dist. by United Feature Syndicate, Inc.
5-26 www.comics.com

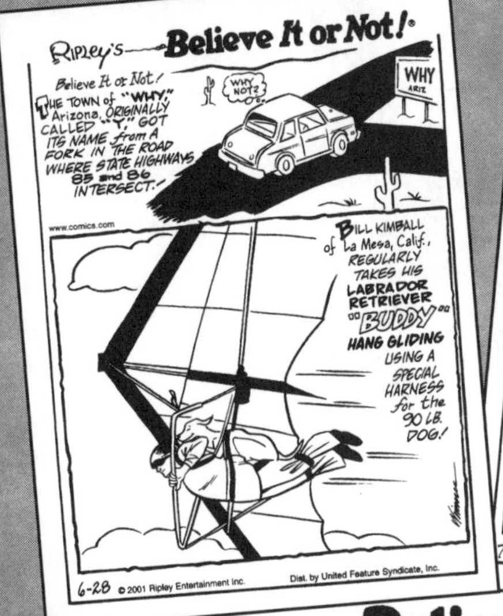

Ripley's Believe It or Not!
Believe It or Not!
THE TOWN of "WHY," Arizona, ORIGINALLY CALLED "Y," GOT ITS NAME from A FORK IN THE ROAD WHERE STATE HIGHWAYS 85 and 86 INTERSECT.
WHY NOT?
WHY ARIZ
www.comics.com
BILL KIMBALL of La Mesa, Calif., REGULARLY TAKES HIS LABRADOR RETRIEVER "BUDDY" HANG GLIDING USING A SPECIAL HARNESS for the 90 LB. DOG!
6-28 © 2001 Ripley Entertainment Inc.
Dist. by United Feature Syndicate, Inc.

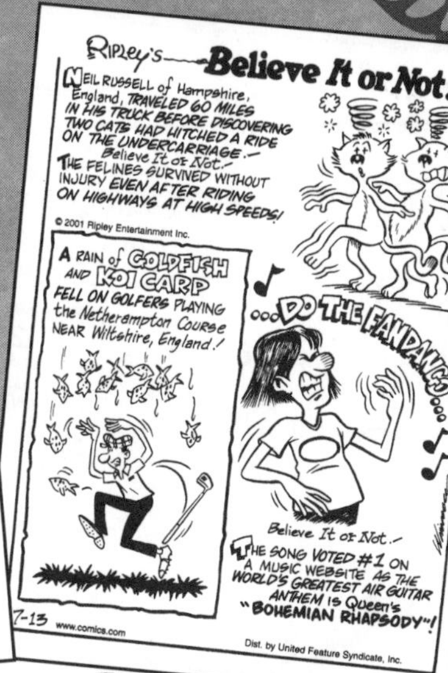

Ripley's Believe It or Not!
NEIL RUSSELL of Hampshire, England, TRAVELED 60 MILES IN HIS TRUCK BEFORE DISCOVERING TWO CATS HAD HITCHED A RIDE ON THE UNDERCARRIAGE.
Believe It or Not.
THE FELINES SURVIVED WITHOUT INJURY EVEN AFTER RIDING ON HIGHWAYS AT HIGH SPEEDS!
© 2001 Ripley Entertainment Inc.
A RAIN of GOLDFISH AND KOI CARP FELL ON GOLFERS PLAYING the Netherampton Course NEAR Wiltshire, England!
...DO THE FANDANGO...
Believe It or Not.
THE SONG VOTED #1 ON A MUSIC WEBSITE AS THE WORLD'S GREATEST AIR GUITAR ANTHEM IS Queen's "BOHEMIAN RHAPSODY"!
7-13 www.comics.com
Dist. by United Feature Syndicate, Inc.

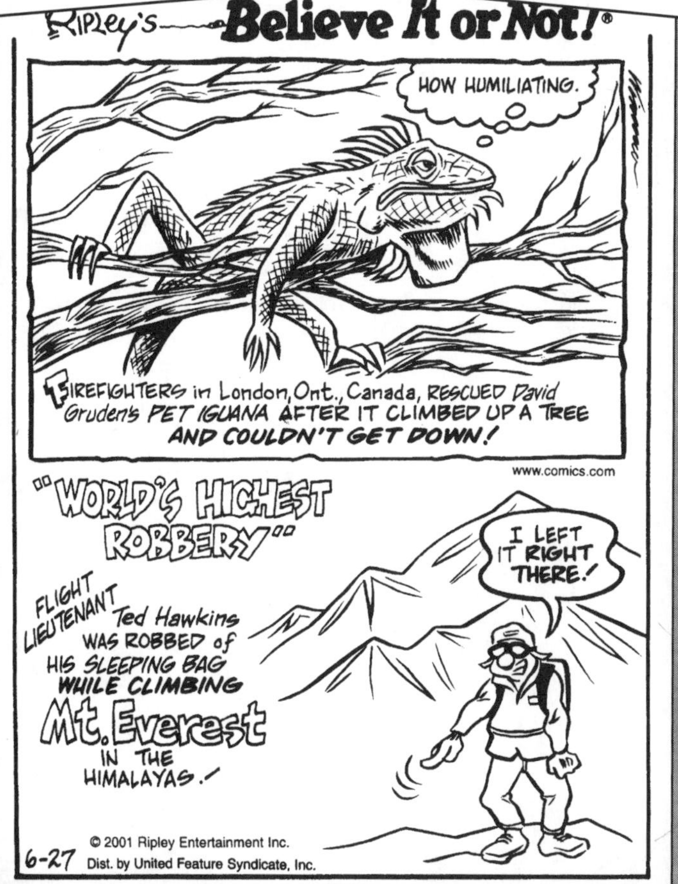

Ripley's Believe It or Not!
HOW HUMILIATING.
FIREFIGHTERS in London, Ont., Canada, RESCUED David Gruden's PET IGUANA AFTER IT CLIMBED UP A TREE AND COULDN'T GET DOWN!
www.comics.com
"WORLD'S HIGHEST ROBBERY"
FLIGHT LIEUTENANT Ted Hawkins WAS ROBBED of HIS SLEEPING BAG WHILE CLIMBING Mt. Everest IN THE HIMALAYAS!
I LEFT IT RIGHT THERE!
6-27 © 2001 Ripley Entertainment Inc.
Dist. by United Feature Syndicate, Inc.

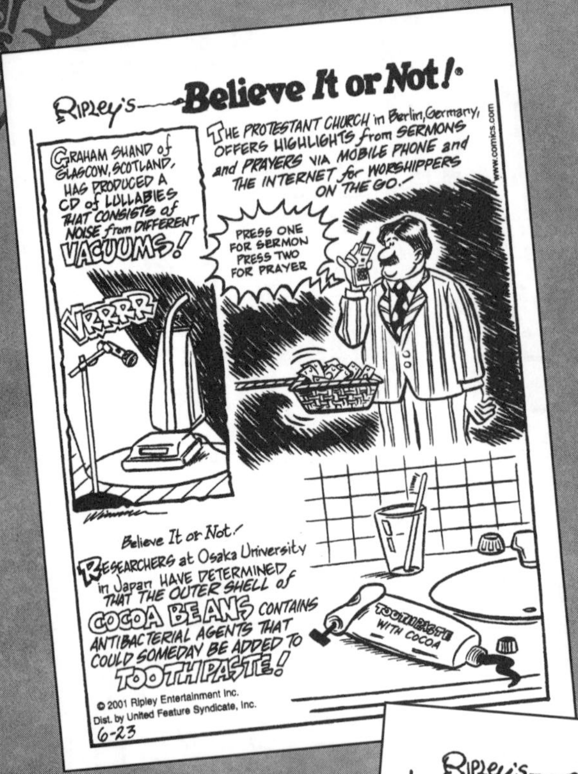
Ripley's Believe It or Not!
Graham Shand of Glasgow, Scotland, has produced a CD of lullabies that consists of noise from different vacuums!
VRRRR
The Protestant Church in Berlin, Germany, offers highlights from sermons and prayers via mobile phone and the internet for worshippers on the go.
Press one for sermon press two for prayer
www.comics.com
Believe It or Not!
Researchers at Osaka University in Japan have determined that the outer shell of cocoa beans contains antibacterial agents that could someday be added to toothpaste!
Toothpaste with cocoa
© 2001 Ripley Entertainment Inc.
Dist. by United Feature Syndicate, Inc.
6-23

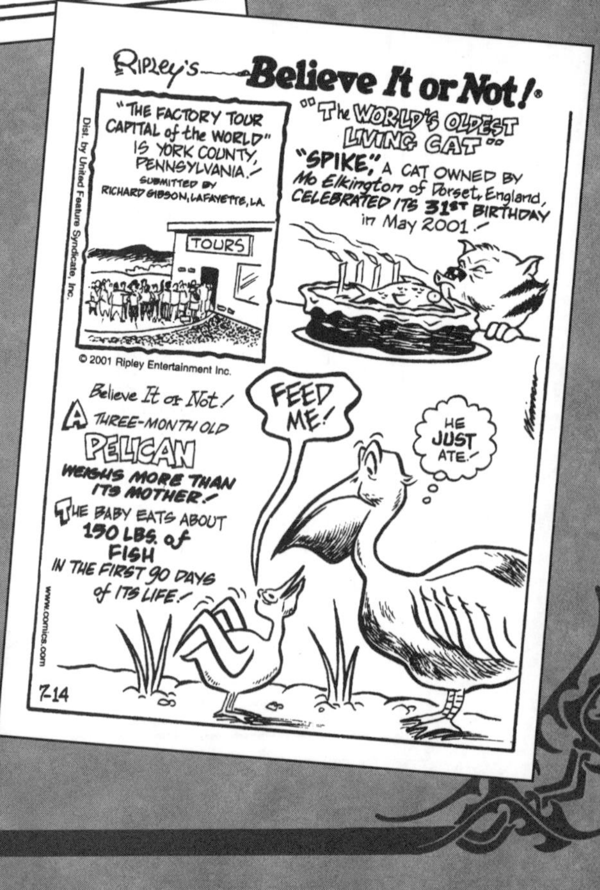
Ripley's Believe It or Not!
"The factory tour capital of the world" is York County, Pennsylvania.
Submitted by Richard Gibson, Lafayette, LA.
TOURS
"The world's oldest living cat"
"Spike," a cat owned by Mo Elkington of Dorset, England, celebrated its 31st birthday in May 2001.
Dist. by United Feature Syndicate, Inc.
© 2001 Ripley Entertainment Inc.
Believe It or Not!
A three-month old pelican weighs more than its mother!
The baby eats about 150 lbs. of fish in the first 90 days of its life!
FEED ME!
HE JUST ATE.
www.comics.com
7-14

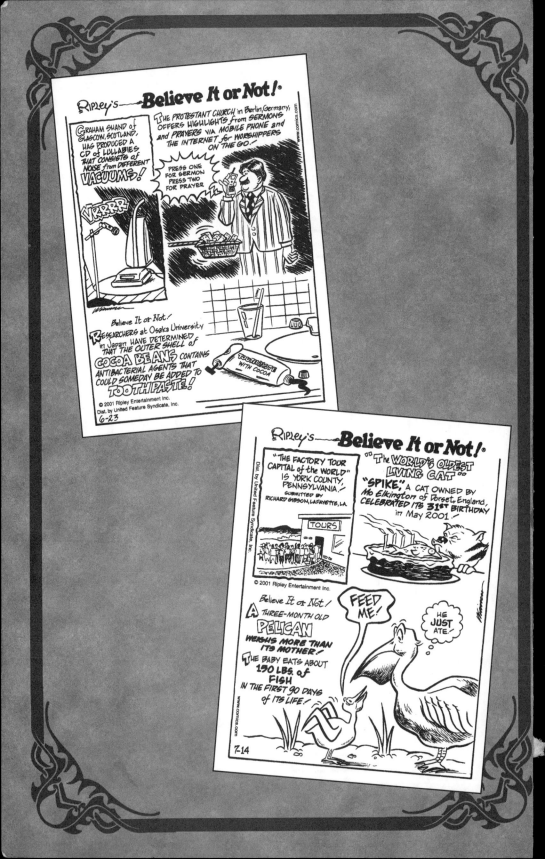